Underage Drinking

Other Books in the Social Issues Firsthand Series:

Underage Drinking

Norah Piehl, Book Editor

GREENHAVEN PRESS
A part of Gale, Cengage Learning

GALE
CENGAGE Learning™

Detroit • New York • San Francisco • New Haven, Conn • Waterville, Maine • London

HV
5135
.U422
2010

GALE
CENGAGE Learning

Christine Nasso, *Publisher*
Elizabeth Des Chenes, *Managing Editor*

© 2010 Greenhaven Press, a part of Gale, Cengage Learning.

Gale and Greenhaven Press are registered trademarks used herein under license.

For more information, contact:
Greenhaven Press
27500 Drake Rd.
Farmington Hills, MI 48331-3535
Or you can visit our Internet site at gale.cengage.com

Articles in Greenhaven Press anthologies are often edited for length to meet page requirements. In addition, original titles of these works are changed to clearly present the main thesis and to explicitly indicate the author's opinion. Every effort is made to ensure that Greenhaven Press accurately reflects the original intent of the authors. Every effort has been made to trace the owners of copyrighted material.

Cover image © Image Source/Corbis.

LIBRARY OF CONGRESS CATALOGING-IN-PUBLICATION DATA

Underage drinking / Norah Piehl, book editor.
    p. cm. -- Social issues firsthand
    Includes bibliographical references and index.
    ISBN 978-0-7377-4799-7 (hbk.)
    1. Youth--Alcohol use--United States--Juvenile literature. 2. Teenagers--Alcohol use--United States. 3. Drinking age--United States--Juvenile literature. 4. Drinking of alcoholic beverages--United States--Juvenile literature. I. Piehl, Norah.
    HV5135.U422 2010
    362.2920835'0973--dc22
                                                                    2009042499

Printed in the United States of America
1 2 3 4 5 6 7 14 13 12 11 10

Contents

Chapter 1: Family Connections

Chapter 2: Drinking on Campus

Foreword

Social issues are often viewed in abstract terms. Pressing challenges such as poverty, homelessness, and addiction are viewed as problems to be defined and solved. Politicians, social scientists, and other experts engage in debates about the extent of the problems, their causes, and how best to remedy them. Often overlooked in these discussions is the human dimension of the issue. Behind every policy debate over poverty, homelessness, and substance abuse, for example, are real people struggling to make ends meet, to survive life on the streets, and to overcome addiction to drugs and alcohol. Their stories are ubiquitous and compelling. They are the stories of everyday people—perhaps your own family members or friends—and yet they rarely influence the debates taking place in state capitols, the national Congress, or the courts.

The disparity between the public debate and private experience of social issues is well illustrated by looking at the topic of poverty. Each year the U.S. Census Bureau establishes a poverty threshold. A household with an income below the threshold is defined as poor, while a household with an income above the threshold is considered able to live on a basic subsistence level. For example, in 2003 a family of two was considered poor if its income was less than $12,015; a family of four was defined as poor if its income was less than $18,810. Based on this system, the bureau estimates that 35.9 million Americans (12.5 percent of the population) lived below the poverty line in 2003, including 12.9 million children below the age of eighteen.

Commentators disagree about what these statistics mean. Social activists insist that the huge number of officially poor Americans translates into human suffering. Even many families that have incomes above the threshold, they maintain, are likely to be struggling to get by. Other commentators insist that the statistics exaggerate the problem of poverty in the United States. Compared to people in developing countries, they point out, most so-called poor families have a high quality of life. As stated by journalist Fidelis Iyebote, "Cars are owned by 70 percent of 'poor' households. . . . Color televisions belong to 97 percent of the 'poor' [and] videocassette recorders belong to nearly 75 percent. . . . Sixty-four percent have microwave ovens, half own a stereo system, and over a quarter possess an automatic dishwasher."

However, this debate over the poverty threshold and what it means is likely irrelevant to a person living in poverty. Simply put, poor people do not need the government to tell them whether they are poor. They can see it in the stack of bills they cannot pay. They are aware of it when they are forced to choose between paying rent or buying food for their children. They become painfully conscious of it when they lose their homes and are forced to live in their cars or on the streets. Indeed, the written stories of poor people define the meaning of poverty more vividly than a government bureaucracy could ever hope to. Narratives composed by the poor describe losing jobs due to injury or mental illness, depict horrific tales of childhood abuse and spousal violence, recount the loss of friends and family members. They evoke the slipping away of social supports and government assistance, the descent into substance abuse and addiction, the harsh realities of life on the streets. These are the perspectives on poverty that are too often omitted from discussions over the extent of the problem and how to solve it.

Greenhaven Press's Social Issues Firsthand series provides a forum for the often-overlooked human perspectives on society's most divisive topics of debate. Each volume focuses on one social issue and presents a collection of ten to sixteen narratives by those who have had personal involvement with the topic. Extra care has been taken to include a diverse range of perspectives. For example, in the volume on adoption, readers will find the stories of birth parents who have made an adoption plan, adoptive parents, and adoptees themselves. After exposure to these varied points of view, the reader will have a clearer understanding that adoption is an intense, emotional experience full of joyous highs and painful lows for all concerned.

The debate surrounding embryonic stem cell research illustrates the moral and ethical pressure that the public brings to bear on the scientific community. However, while nonexperts often criticize scientists for not considering the potential negative impact of their work, ironically the public's reaction against such discoveries can produce harmful results as well. For example, although the outcry against embryonic stem cell research in the United States has resulted in fewer embryos being destroyed, those with Parkinson's, such as actor Michael J. Fox, have argued that prohibiting the development of new stem cell lines ultimately will prevent a timely cure for the disease that is killing Fox and thousands of others.

Each book in the series contains several features that enhance its usefulness, including an in-depth introduction, an annotated table of contents, bibliographies for further research, a list of organizations to contact, and a thorough index. These elements—combined with the poignant voices of people touched by tragedy and triumph—make the Social Issues Firsthand series a valuable resource for research on today's topics of political discussion.

Introduction

Eighteen-year-old Ben knows—from personal experience—the difference between pinot noir and cabernet sauvignon, between ale and lager. His parents, who often enjoy a beer or glass of wine with dinner, believe in educating Ben about the pleasures and responsibilities of drinking alcohol. As long as he can remember, Ben has been able to try a sip of whatever his parents were drinking, even when he was little and did not really care for the taste. As soon as Ben turned sixteen, his parents let him have a single glass of wine with dinner, and the family now enjoys trying different wines together. Ben's parents hope that when their son soon leaves for college, his understanding of good wine and beer and his ability to drink moderately will help him resist the pressure to binge drink.

After high school graduation, Ben attends a house party hosted by his friend Emma's parents. The hosts collect partygoers' car keys at the door and provide tents in the backyard where kids can stay until morning. Although Emma's parents do not supply any alcohol, there is an understanding that kids can—and will—bring their own booze and drink in a safe environment. At the party, Ben does not drink much, but some of the kids do—and when the backyard party gets a little loud, one of the neighbors calls the police. Under their town ordinance, Emma's parents are arrested for hosting a party where underage alcohol consumption is allowed—and before they are assessed a hefty fine, they are informed that if anyone had been hurt or killed after the party, the hosts could have been held criminally responsible.

Although the above examples are fictitious, they reflect the reality of two recent trends that are shaping how, and where, teenagers drink in the United States. Although some parents are choosing to adopt a European model of educating their children and teens about alcohol by allowing them to drink at home, an increasing number of state and local ordinances are cracking down on so-called supervised parties, hosted by adults who understand that alcohol may be consumed by underage drinkers on their property. So where do parents draw the line? Can home be a safe place for teens to learn to drink responsibly? Or is abstinence the only answer?

Organizations seeking to control underage drinking frequently point out that overall rates of teenage drinking have declined over the past fifteen years. According to a 1991 University of Michigan study, 81 percent of middle- and high-school students had had at least one alcoholic drink in their lives; when the study was repeated in 2007, only 58 percent of the same age group had ever had a drink.

Those young people who do drink, however, are increasingly likely to drink to excess; according to a recent study at the Harvard School of Public Health, 26 percent of college students who drink have blacked out at least once, while 13 percent have suffered an "accident or injury" due to drinking. Both figures have nearly doubled since a similar survey was taken in the mid-twentieth century.

Theories on how to reduce the culture of binge drinking, especially on college campuses, vary, but studies at Penn State University and the University of Maryland in 2008 seem to suggest that abstinence prior to starting college is the best policy: in the Maryland study, students who did not drink in high school at all consumed an average of only 1.8 alcoholic beverages each time they drank during their first year in college, while their classmates who had more drinking experience averaged five drinks per drinking occasion.

Anti–underage drinking activists have adopted various strategies to combat rates of teen drinking over the years, ranging from positive peer pressure to scare tactics to leadership training. Both activists and parents, however, have realized over time that although total abstinence is an admirable goal, it might not be a realistic one. For some parents, the solution is to provide "safe parties" at homes where teens can drink in an environment with parental supervision, where (in theory) bingeing can be controlled, accidents can be prevented, and driving under the influence can be avoided altogether.

Activist organizations such as Mothers Against Drunk Driving, however, have sought to control such so-called supervised parties by lobbying for passage of state and local "social host" liability laws, which hold homeowners civilly or criminally responsible when underage drinking occurs on their property. As of 2008, twenty-three states have social host laws in place, the majority having been passed since 2000. Individual counties and municipalities can also pass their own social host laws, which often carry stiffer penalties or provide stricter regulations than state laws.

Although property owners are usually criminally prosecuted when a crime (such as drunk driving or death) occurs as a direct result of a party held at their home, most social host laws can be enforced and the violators prosecuted in either civil or criminal court even if no other crimes occur. In many jurisdictions, homeowners can be prosecuted even if they are not at home when the incident occurs, meaning that people can be arrested for a party that happens when they are out of town—even out of the country.

Supporters of social host laws argue that they provide important safeguards, that even well-meaning parents cannot know everything that happens at a "supervised" party: "Parents don't even know what is going on in their basements," commented a police officer in Stratford, Connecticut, which, according to *Time* magazine, passed a social host ordinance in 2003. Organizations such as Mothers Against Drunk Driving, which actively encourages its members to introduce similar ordinances in their own towns, argue that such laws hold whole families and communities responsible for underage drinking, not just the individuals who procure the alcohol. A

2009 editorial in the *Boston Globe* expresses hope that enforcement of Massachusetts's state social host laws can help prevent deaths like those of two teenage girls who, in separate incidents separated by only a couple of months, drowned after wandering away from house parties.

Proponents of family privacy, however, are concerned that overly restrictive social host laws may violate family and personal privacy. Most social host ordinances do contain exceptions for parents who serve their own children alcohol in their homes, but privacy advocates have expressed concern of what would constitute "reasonable cause" for police to enter and search a home if they suspect a minor is drinking, even with parents. There is also the philosophical question of should government regulate what many families consider to be private decisions about how to raise their children. One city council member quoted in the *Time* magazine article argues that social host legislation "usurps parents' rights to raise and manage children in the way they see fit in their own home." Such ordinances may especially affect families like Ben's, who believe that educating their own son about alcohol is the best way to prepare him for a lifetime of responsible drinking.

Is it possible to make distinctions between the family that serves an underage member an occasional glass of wine or beer as part of a family dinner or celebration and the family that hosts a supervised party for their children and their friends? Yes, argues addiction expert Stanton Peele, who has written books on addiction, including *Addiction-Proof Your Child*. In this book, Peele draws a distinction between permissive child rearing—which often results in high-risk behavior—and authoritative parenting, which sets firm boundaries but allows young people great leeway for independence within those boundaries.

In the two examples that opened this introduction, Emma's parents would fall closer to Peele's definition of permissive parenting, in which the children's desires dictate the parents' actions. Ben's parents would fit into the authoritative parenting model: "Modeling appropriate and responsible drinking, and expecting your children to behave the same way, embodies the authoritative style," writes Peele. Integrating moderate alcohol consumption into regular family rituals and celebrations, Peele argues, is the perfect middle ground, neither treating alcohol as a "forbidden fruit" that's off-limits until they reach a certain legal age nor elevating it to be the centerpiece of a parent-approved (but increasingly illegal) teens-only party.

Social Issues Firsthand: Underage Drinking presents personal narratives about underage drinking from a variety of perspectives. The debate about how best to control the binge-centered culture of underage and college drinking will likely rage for years to come.

SOCIAL ISSUES
FIRSTHAND

CHAPTER 1

Family Connections

Forgive and Forget

Koren Zailckas

By the time she was in high school, Koren Zailckas was already a problem drinker. She began drinking heavily at age fourteen and continued drinking—often to frightening extremes—for the next decade.

In her best-selling memoir, Smashed, *from which this story is taken, Zailckas relates her own experiences with alcohol as a way to illustrate the growing problem of girls and young women abusing alcohol more heavily, and at younger ages, than ever before. In this excerpt, Zailckas describes one of her early drinking exploits with a friend during a family summer vacation. The story illustrates two of Zailckas's themes: the dangerous culture of binge drinking among young women and the tendency of parents to look the other way. Here, Zailckas's parents catch her drinking for the first time, and their surprisingly calm reaction seems to foreshadow their later tendencies to believe the best of their daughter even in the face of overwhelming evidence to the contrary.*

In addition to Smashed, *Koren Zailckas has contributed to several publications, including the* New York Times, Glamour, Jane, *and* Seventeen. *She has another memoir,* Enraged, *forthcoming. She grew up in Massachusetts and attended Syracuse University in New York.*

The first time my parents catch me drinking is during the summer of 1995, in Ocean City, Maryland. Ocean City is the perfect place to get caught red-handed, what with its miles of boardwalk and green, plastic, mini-golf turf, its snack bars smelling of crab cakes, and the saltwater breeze carrying the screams of children as they plunge down waterslides. The setting means everyone involved can write the whole mess off as situational. It makes my drinking look like the exception as opposed to the norm, a seasonal recreation only slightly more hazardous than body surfing or searing in the noon sun without Coppertone.

There are two motivations for our trip: my father's promotion and my injury. Sometime in May, my father receives a raise at the technological corporation where he works. Around the same time, I topple down the basement stairs and tear a ligament in my knee. The sequence of the two events seems significant to me. The whole world is rising, while I fall.

After my accident, I visit two doctors and three specialists. The last of them is an orthopedic surgeon at Emerson Hospital, a man I later dub Dr. Fix-It, who schedules me for reconstructive surgery in August.

Too Normal

I pass out on the examining table the day I receive the prognosis. I am shifting my weight on the parchment while Dr. Fix-It is describing his plans to harvest a portion of my hamstring and insert it into my knee. He is pointing out exactly where on the X-ray board, where my bones are lit up like a slide show of his recent trip to Fiji, and yet all I can think is, *There is some mistake, that skeleton can't possibly be mine.*

The bones are just too regular, like a stock photo from *Gray's Anatomy.* I'd assumed that inside, I'd look as dark and knotty as I feel. I was hoping the X-ray board could show me the injury I feel so deeply, a hurt that justifies the framework I've been using for living. For the past year, I've told myself that I'm drinking and smoking and otherwise acting delinquent because high school has dealt me a shitty hand, that I am winning neither popularity nor academic contests, that I am unsure and insufficient—in a word, *sick.* But there on the X-ray, I'm faced with proof that, deep down, I'm sturdy; even full-grown Dr. Fix-It says so. It is the notion of health, not injury, that makes me ill. It forces me to lean over and put my head between my knees.

I spend the rest of the school year hobbling up stairs and out of cars, never certain when my knee will submit and give out under me. Without my intricate agenda of after school activities, I give in to self-imposed quarantine. I spend afternoons paging through stolen library books in the backyard's canvas lawn chair. Evenings, I keep vigil in the living room in front of infomercials.

Recapturing the Past

In an effort to cheer me up, my mother proposes a vacation. I propose Ocean City. We spent three consecutive summers there, when I was five, six, and seven, and I've retained every second of each of them. I can remember burrowing for sand crabs in the wet sand down by the surf, letting them squirm to their deaths in a pebble-filled tank because I loved them too much to liberate them. I remember the boardwalk, where my mother bought me a T-shirt with a beaded hem that jingled when I walked. I remember the length of beach where I played catch with my father, way past my usual bedtime, and the way my hands looked when they slow-motion-grasped for the glow-in-the-dark ball. I remember the name of every resort on the strip—The Golden Sands, The Palm, The Prism—and the mirrored windows that made each one look as sunny as the sky. I remember mornings that I sat on a condo carpet, eating Cabbage Patch Kids cereal, which was the type of sugary snack that was forbidden at home, and savoring each candy-coated puff on my tongue like a gemstone far too precious to swallow.

To other people, Ocean City may be a tumbledown summer town with a name that ought to be implied. But to me, it's always represented hedonism.

I imagine my parents associate Ocean City with unity, with the years before I hit adolescence and became too mean and moody to take, because they agree to my destination quickly and resolutely. My mother even suggests I bring Natalie, who is home for two months on summer break, because the condo she's rented is big enough for us to have our own room. It feels like her final attempt to coax a smile out of me. . . .

Sneaking Out

The bedroom Natalie and I share turns out to be more like our own little apartment. It has its own bathroom, a queen-sized bed under a tufted comforter, and a sitting area where yellowed paperbacks are stacked beside a transistor TV. We fold our swimsuits into the room's white dresser and spread our arsenal of curling irons across the paint-chipped surface of the nightstand. Natalie parts the window's lace curtains, and we stand for a few minutes in front of it, awed by the condominiums that shoot up thirty stories high over the Coastal Highway. My parents' room faces the beach, and ours faces the street, and we prefer it that way.

We wait three nights to push out the screen and boost ourselves out of the window.

We started sneaking out of Natalie's house a month ago. We'd spend whole days drafting our escape plans, testing to see which hinges whined, which floorboards creaked, and gathering devices we might use to prop, resist, and muffle them. At night, we'd wait for the TV to fall silent in Natalie's parents' bedroom, and we'd silently stuff Natalie's bed and my sleeping bag with stuffed animals and sweaters. Then we'd tip-toe down the staircase, roll open the garage door, and sprint to where the driveway meets the street.

Most nights, the joy of the prison break was enough. We didn't need any plans, aside from walking the culs-de-sac like two ghosts, taunting the neighbors' tied-up Labradors, kicking bits of gravel and sharing cigarettes.

We'd learned to stay in the neighborhood after the night we hitchhiked to a party near Natalie's boarding school, where we drank Heineken and listened to a band, and nearly got stuck there without anyone to drive us home. At three A.M., we'd finally agreed to pay an older boy fifteen dollars in exchange for a ride. He had a summer job as an ice-cream man, and he drove us home in his singing white truck.

Years later, when my parents ask if I used to drink and sneak out because I wanted to test their boundaries, I'll say yes, even though that was never my aim. I won't know how to tell them it was a suicidal impulse that drove me out windows. I had a curious *It's a Wonderful Life*–like compulsion to explore what my house, or my life, would look like without me in it.

On the Town

Natalie and I find a stand in our condo closet. It's a fold-out deal with metal legs and canvas rungs, and whoever put it there probably intended it for supporting suitcases or drying beach towels. But we see its full potential. Natalie unfolds it beneath the bedroom window and steps back to whisper, "After you." I position one foot on each of the metal legs and stand there, spread-eagle, for a moment of breath-catching before I grab both sides of the window frame and hoist myself out, one inch at a time.

We don't speak a word until we hit the pavement in the condo's parking lot. That is the divide, the predetermined finish line, and once we cross it we're free. There, we slip our feet back into our sandals and let out our pent-up laughter. All around us, the strip is illuminated with neon signs and headlights. People are everywhere, in cars, leaning out of hotel windows, roaming the sidewalks as they drink from foam-sheathed beer cans.

I feel like I did when I was younger, when my sister and I would linger on the stairs in our nightgowns during my parents' adults-only dinner parties, listening to the muffled laughter and the chiming sound of my father hitting his wineglass with a spoon. Tonight, the Coastal Highway confirms that old suspicion: There is a whole world that takes shape during the hours I'm asleep.

Across the street from the condo, Natalie and I wait for the trolley car, trying to decide if the ten dollars wadded up in our pockets is enough to feed the fare machine for two round-trip tickets. It is. When the trolley pulls up, we choose seats in the far back, which we know to be the most desirable spots on a school bus. We ride for thirty minutes, and fifty blocks.

Earlier in the day we met a guy behind the counter of the Pizza Palace who directed us to the part of town where the college kids hang out. They are waiters and lifeguards, he said, who rent entire houses on their own. Listening to him, I couldn't help but envision the staff kids in *Dirty Dancing*, the way they embraced booze, sex, and rock music like life, love, and the hunt for happiness. I sit in the trolley's grooved plastic seat, imagining I'm Baby—only I won't have to carry a watermelon the way she did to get into a party; I sense that being a girl is its own free pass inside.

A Version of Myself

Natalie and I aren't sure where to go once we step off the trolley. It's my idea to take off our sandals and wander down the beach, past all the darkened resorts that have beach chairs stacked in the sand. We aren't walking anywhere in particular, but Natalie keeps urging me to move faster because it's her nature. I trail behind her, watching the red tip of her cigarette move to and from her mouth, and the way the wet sand erases her footprints as soon as she makes them.

Down the beach, we see a campfire. In the dark, we can spot its orange spark, like a meteor, from a long way off. As we tread closer, we can see the empty beer bottles in the sand and the keg on ice in a trash can, a web of people settled around it. It looks like any cigarette or beer ad: a tight-knit circle of strangers made friends by atmosphere alone. Girls huddle on driftwood while boys drop kelp down their blouses. Flames brighten their faces. Steely waves crash at their backs.

It feels good to give myself over to that formula. It is like the type of extra credit where you get points for just showing up. The kids on the beach don't care that they don't know Natalie and me. A boy stands to offer us his space on a blanket. Someone else brings us beer in clear plastic cups. They welcome us into their circle, no questions asked, and we don't have to work for any of it.

The funny thing about that unconditional stamp of approval is that it makes me act less like myself. For all intents and purposes, it should make me more comfortable being regular old Koren—idiosyncratic, a bit phobic in groups, but a decent girl if you get to know her. But instead, I, too, conform to a beer-ad version of myself. I kick off my shoes and pirouette in the sand. I agree to drink beer from a funnel, even though I know the boy channeling it through will pour too fast, and I will end up wearing the thick tar of beer and wet sand. When Natalie and the other girls strip down to their underwear, I do, too. I ride a boogie board in my undershirt and white cotton panties, and don't care when the salt water makes my skin show through.

At the time, I write off these behaviors as a need to adapt. I don't want to stand out as a high-school girl, the type of baby who can't keep up with buxom sorority girls from Southern universities. I want to prove that I can funnel as much beer as they can, that I can unflinchingly take the same lascivious looks in the dark.

Later, I'll be able to see that this is how it all starts. I concede to shifting my personality, just a hair, to observe the standards I think the situation calls for. From now on, every time I drink, I'll enhance various aspects of myself, willing myself into a state where I am a little bit brighter, funnier, more outgoing, or vibrant. The process will be so incremental that I'll have no gauge of how much it will change me. I will wake up one day in my twenties like a skewed TV screen on which the hues are all wrong. My subtleties will be exaggerated and my overtones will be subdued. My entire personality will be off-color.

Another Party

Natalie and I cut and run again the next night. It's the same escape route: over the stand, out the window, and down the strip on the trolley. This time, we head for a party in a large, stilted cottage a few blocks west of the beach. At the campfire the night before, a boy wrote the address in ballpoint pen on Natalie's forearm. . . .

Three beers and twelve watercolors later I go downstairs to find Natalie. It isn't that I have forgotten about her; she has always been there in my mind, like a telephone ringing in the background. I feel guilty for neglecting her. I imagine she's downstairs on the porch, smoking a Marlboro and delivering a sermon on Kurt Cobain conspiracy theories, which is her version of small talk. Hopefully, she's done some kissing, too, with Wally, in which case she won't be fed up with waiting for me. Either way, I'm obliged to go downstairs and pick her up.

But Natalie isn't on the porch. She isn't in the TV room, the game room, or the kitchen, either. I know because I am gripping Greg's hand and tugging him from one room to the next. I can't imagine where Natalie is, or why she would leave me. That's the big thing: I don't understand how she could abandon *me* in a house full of strangers, with dawn about to break. I imagine my parents getting up in a few hours, making breakfast and going about the business of preparing for the beach; sooner or later they will discover our empty room and the towels we have stuffed between our sheets.

Greg decides we should check Wally's room, and relief washes over me. It occurs to me that the night has already been going in the direction of a double date: The boys have paired off with us, to steal whatever couple time they can. . . .

Finding Natalie

I find Natalie in an armchair, looking wilted. She is conscious, but barely. Her head is bowed forward and her eyes, rolled way back, divulge only the whites. It is a look she once perfected at a rock club, when she pretended to pass out in the pit so we could watch the band from a better vantage point backstage. I can't help hoping she is faking again.

Around her are guys and a few girls, jumbled around a coffee table and on a paisley sofa, playing cards and sipping beer. A joint, the first I have ever seen, burns in a scalloped clay ashtray. I don't need anyone to tell me it isn't a cigarette. Somehow the smoke just smells green.

I go to Natalie's armchair and grab one of her legs with both hands, rattling it loosely, the way I might rouse someone from an afternoon nap. With the white flesh of her thigh in my hand, I realize she is wearing someone else's clothes. Her jeans and polo shirt have been replaced with blue mesh shorts and a white undershirt.

I don't even bother asking Natalie where her clothes are because it's clear that she can't speak. Instead, I stand up and spin around to face the people on the sofa; I ask them where the *f---* her clothes are.

"She threw up on them," a girl with a throaty voice says. She holds the joint between the nails of her thumb and her index finger and examines it like a tiny bug she is thinking of squashing.

"Natalie?" I lean over and shake her by the shoulders, too hard now, but I can't help it. I am desperate to wake her in the way people are desperate to revive their dead lovers in made-for-TV movies. I don't care if I look melodramatic. This is the closest I've ever come to seeing a corpse.

"*Natalie?*" When I call her name in my trumpet scream, the green half-moons of her eyes roll in my direction.

"*You f---ing bitch,*" she says and leans over as if to spit on me, but drool just rolls down one side of her chin in a glistening tear.

A guy says, "This might be a good time to get her out of here?"

Greg hauls Natalie out of the armchair and onto her feet. He has to hold her by the waist to keep her upright, while I hunt for her shoes. She stands there like a ski jumper, leaning her head into his chest with her legs locked too far out behind her. She lets out another string of profanities when I lean down to put on her flip-flops.

"*F---ing bitch-ass dirty slut.*"

She drops to her hands and knees on the floor, and her shoulders start to tremble like she is going to be sick.

Someone says plainly, "Get her out of here." . . .

Trapped

At any minute, I imagine my parents will hit the bar on their alarm clock. My mom will go to the bathroom and start the shower spray; my ten-year-old sister will turn on cartoons; my dad will go out to buy bagels. There is no way I can stuff Natalie through the window in her condition, and if we use the front door, my parents will instantly know about the beach, the boys, and the booze.

I am stuck in this situation, and the feeling that follows that realization is the same dread and shortness of breath I felt the time I got wedged behind a basement bookshelf I wasn't strong enough to move. I am trapped and there is no way out; I can't keep that knowledge to myself any longer.

I unleashed a string of confessions on Greg. I tell him that I am not eighteen or seventeen, but fifteen, and that I am actually staying with my parents and not an aunt. These are small distinctions, but to me they feel indispensable, like pronouns, without which he has no hope of understanding my language.

He says, "Don't worry about your parents. They'll be mad at first, but so what? The worst they can do is ground you. It's not the end of the world."

The sun is creeping up the sky like a bug on a wall, and all around us people are climbing into their cars to go to work. I look at Greg, and notice for the first time that he is practically crawling out of his skin, anxious to go home and, presumably, sleep before his shift at the surf shop. He, too, looks younger in the sunlight, less collegiate, more like a boy I barely know.

The trolley pulls up and I thrust Natalie onto it.

Getting Caught

The ride back to the condo is unbearable. Natalie vomits twice, and each time I struggle to hide her from the bus driver, who is watching us knowingly in his rearview mirror. I lean over and pretend to tie my shoelaces while I cover the puddles with stray newspapers. Whole families get on, carting canvas bags filled with black beach towels and sunblock. Businessmen drink coffee from foam cups and peruse *USA Today*. Construction workers clutch their scuffed hard hats in their laps. Some of them look at us with disgust, and others offer commentary, like "Friend had a rough night, eh?"

No one offers to help. No one pulls the emergency brake and shouts for a doctor. To them, we are no crisis; we're a joke. Their smirks reflect my most grisly apprehensions. We are ingrates, prime examples of godless, suburban white girls, defects in the knit of society.

When we get back, Natalie is still too drunk to climb through the window. I am forced to do the unthinkable. I cringe, and carry her in through the condo's front door.

When I lead her to bed she seems to wake up a bit, as though she has amnesia and the bed is the only thing she recognizes. She barely responds when I call her by name, but somehow the sight of the lace pillowcases flips a switch in her brain that says, *Sleep, sleep here, sleep now.* I let her crawl in between the covers without even bothering to remove the heaps of towels we had skillfully sculpted only hours earlier. I change quietly into a nightgown and curl beside her. I put my head on her shoulder so I can monitor her breathing. As far as I can tell, the rising and falling of her chest seems regular.

I don't have a chance to doze off before my mother materializes in the bedroom doorway.

"Koren," she whispers. I can see she has already changed into a beach cover-up and a wide straw hat. "We're going down to the pool. Please come down after you've rested; we'd like to talk to you."

"Shit," I shout, after I hear the front door close behind her.

Learning the Truth

Hours pass, and I am filled with the same sense of doom I felt in seventh grade, when Mrs. Kent sent me to the principal's office when I refused to read aloud. F--- Greg for telling me this isn't the end of the world. It is the end of *my* world, the one in which I am an admittedly mopey teenager, but still the firstborn daughter, a decent student but for math and science, and the apple of my daddy's eye.

Rest? Who was my mother kidding? My eyes burn with exhaustion, but I can't sleep. I keep imagining my head on a chopping block, instead of a too-thin hotel pillow. I try to evaluate the incriminating evidence. Until I decide how much my parents actually know, I can't draft a speech in my defense. My mind spins. When I close my eyes, I feel like I'm nose-diving into a spiral descent. I'm not hungover, but I run to the bathroom and throw up.

Natalie joins me a few minutes later, and we take turns holding one another's hair and heaving into the bowl. We flush, and she tries her best to tell me what happened. Alcohol has muddled the details, so she fills in the blanks as best she can. Wally brought her to his room, bolted the door, and tried to put his hands down her pants. She escaped his grasp narrowly and unharmed, but she didn't feel like waiting on the porch, and she didn't want to mount the stairs to the studio and disrupt my time alone with Greg. So she went for a walk. She walked along the beach where we had been the night before, and when a group of guys called out to her, she joined them on their deck. She chugged what she thought was a jumbo-sized plastic cup of beer, but when she was halfway finished, it occurred to her that it might have been liquor. She also smoked what she thought was a joint, but the contents were whiter, she said, and it occurred to her that it might have been angel dust.

My stomach does another revolution, and I think I might throw up again. The scenario Natalie has described is even worse than the one I imagined. In my heart of hearts, I had thought we'd both only had a few beers. I thought she had just been "a two-beer queer," which was a term she always used to describe me when I got drunk off of very little. But the truth is laced with liquor, boys, and drugs. There is no way I can relay it to my parents, who, I imagine, wait impatiently by the pool, already burning in the one o'clock sun.

I ask Natalie if she's okay, and it's a leading question. I am trying to make her agree so I can stop my own nauseous feeling, the one that tells me this is my fault. I say, "Natalie, nobody *did anything* to you, did they?"

"I don't think so," she says, and her forehead crinkles up, as though she's considering the possibility for the first time. "But then, I don't remember everything."

It will be years before I know the horror and shame that make Natalie cringe. I will have to experience it myself before

I can understand that there are two parts of the mind that constrain memory after nights like this: one that wants to dig it up, and another that wants to push it deeper down. In college, I will learn about boys and blackouts firsthand, about the way the things you can't remember can terrorize you.

I lean my head over the toilet bowl and passionately ralph.

Facing the Music

Around two o'clock I trudge in the direction of the hotel pool, like a dead girl walking, thinking I can't possibly put it off any longer. I resolve to accept my punishment. Hopefully, my parents' backlash will be quick and painless, a kind of lethal injection, my social life ended abruptly at the hands of the state.

I spot them sitting at a flimsy poolside patio table. The morning's clouds have blown off, and behind them the day is flawlessly blue. In the pool, children buoy to the surface on red foam boards. Teenaged girls, who look exactly like me, stretch out, catlike, on lawn chairs, reading fashion magazines, and applying oil to the skin beneath their bikini strings. Waiters are everywhere, carrying piña coladas in sweaty glasses. It is an unlikely location for my first lecture about drinking.

When I get to the table, I look down and see a glass of beer resting in front of chair number three.

"I hope you don't mind," my father says. "We went ahead and ordered for you."

"A Fraction of the Truth"

I decide to tell a fraction of the truth. It will become something I will tell my parents for years in times of distress. I like to think of it as the-whole-truth-and-nothing-but-the-truth's second cousin; they may not share all the same physical characteristics, but there is no denying they're related.

Years later, it's hard to remember the precise story that I tell them. But it is exactly that—a *story*. I shift various facts around like squares on a Rubik's Cube, in the hope of aligning the details. They only get more jumbled when my parents ask me to repeat them.

The night sounds like a fairy tale by the time I am through reconstructing it. Natalie and I left the house at midnight because we couldn't fall asleep. We walked along the beach to tire ourselves, enjoying the mist and the moon and the damp sand under our feet. We found a party somewhere along the breaking waves, and it was not unlike the Mad Hatter's tea party: Everyone was gathered around a campfire, singing songs, raising their glasses, and switching seats. Someone offered us something from a keg, which we drank to gauge the mystical effects it would have on us.

The narrative is straight out of *Alice in Wonderland*, right down to the bottle marked DRINK ME. My father is repressing a look that says, *Off with her head*.

He asks how many beers I drank.

"Two, only two." Saying things twice always seems to substantiate them.

He asks if I've ever had a drink before.

"No," I lie. "Never."

My mother asks what Natalie drank.

Since I'll never know, I guess and say, "Four beers."

Her look is dubious.

"Koren, she smells like *hard alcohol*." My mother is a bloodhound. She could make a living sniffing out contraband in luggage at customs.

I shrug and say she might have had hard alcohol. I add, "It's not like I was watching her every second."

New Responsibilities

My mother gasps.

She says, "Listen, *little girl*." It is the first time in the conversation that she has raised her voice, and whenever she calls me "little girl" I know she means business. "Natalie is your friend. You two are supposed to look out for each other. *Particularly* if you're going to be drinking." She doesn't need to add that I shouldn't have been drinking. We both know, at this point, that it is extraneous to the conversation.

What she says makes sense, and ultimately, it is the one real lesson I take away from that lecture by the pool: *During times of booze, girls are responsible for nurturing one another.* When she says it, an image flashes through my mind of Jodie Foster in *Foxes*, pouring coffee and cornflakes for her girl-friends after a night of too much Scotch and too many quaaludes. If drinking is like playing grown-up or playing house, somebody has to be the mother. And the fact that my own mother says this makes the knowledge feel all the more sacred, like a bond passed down by women through the ages. I add it to my list of drinking commandments, alongside *Thou shalt select a designated driver.*

"There weren't any boys involved, were there?" I know she is really asking if there was any sex involved.

If girls need to defend each other while they drink, sex is the threat we need to protect one another from. The thing I am discovering about girldom is, in the end, nobody cares if you are a drunk, an anorexic, a runaway, a dropout, a dope fiend, or a psychotic. These things aren't regaled, but they are allowed. With the right amount of therapy or religion or pharmaceuticals, they can be remedied and passed off as life stages. That is, as long as you are still a virgin. To be a whore is to be unsalvageable.

"No. God, no," I half-mouth the words in a way that suggests the scenario is so far-fetched it doesn't merit sound. But secretly, I am wondering if something other than vomit impelled Natalie out of her clothes and into those gym shorts.

It wasn't too long ago that Natalie and I rented the movie *Kids*, and I haven't been able to forget the look on Chloë Sevigny's face when her character is raped while she is passed out on a sofa, drunk and high. The camera captures the whole horrifying scene, and it gave me nightmares for months after I saw it. I could not stop thinking of how each thrust sent the pleather couch squeaking. The boy had bent her legs so far back over her head, they looked as though they'd snap off at her hips.

Optimism or Denial?

My parents never say the words "get-out-of-jail-free card," but that's what this is. As a first-time offender, I escape any real punishment. They make it clear that I will be severely sorry if they catch me drinking again. They establish what addiction counselors call a "No-Use" rule. I am not, under any circumstances, allowed to drink alcohol outside of their company before I graduate from high school. They say, "If you're curious about alcohol, that's fine, but you'll drink it with us." I am more than welcome to have half a glass of wine with dinner.

My parents seem almost relieved to get the discussion out of the way. I get the sense that they've been waiting to catch me drinking, the same way they've been waiting to catch me kissing some boy in the den. To them, it is just another version of the birds and the bees, a conversation they've been waiting for years to spring on me, holding off until I was developed enough to pass for old enough. For the most part, this lesson about alcohol strikes me as more discourse to file away with panty liners and antiperspirant. It is the type of embarrassing lecture that makes all of us uncomfortable.

They are generous with my punishment. I am grounded for a week, which means little in the grand scheme of things. I routinely get more jail time for a failing a math test or harassing my sister.

Their real charity, though, is in terms of Natalie. I'd just assumed this would be one of those situations where my mother called Natalie's mother, the way she used to when we were younger and she caught us watching R-rated movies. Up until this point, it seemed to be the preferred parental way of dealing with things—everyone rehashing the events and comparing notes out of obligation, outrage, or guilt. Instead, they decide to let Natalie tell her parents herself. I think they do it because we are old enough to be trusted as active participants in our retribution. It will take me years to see it for what it is: embarrassment and the desire to pretend the whole thing never happened.

That will be the thing about my parents. From the outside, they will come off as suspicious as hell. They will dutifully set and enforce curfews. They will ask where I'm going, and with whom. They'll keep asking who'll be there, how long I'll be gone, and how I'm getting back. My father will hug me when I come home at night, as if to check my breath for alcohol. My mother will linger in my room too long when she is putting away laundry; she'll slide her fingers along the bottoms of my drawers as if she's checking for drug-filled plastic Baggies. But when it comes down to the hard evidence, the material proof sitting right in front of them in sunglasses and sweatpants, the very portrait of hungover, they will choose optimism. They'll believe in the best in me. And years later, they'll believe in the best in my sister.

Every parent would rather believe that their child abstains—from sex, drugs, booze, and violence, all the cultish impulses.

Mother and Son

Toren Volkmann and Chris Volkmann

Overcoming alcohol addiction is a personal decision and a personal struggle. However, as anyone who has gone through a twelve-step program or other alcoholism recovery program can attest, both the disease and its cure have deeper roots in the alcoholic's family life.

The first of the following excerpts takes the form of an e-mail written by Toren Volkmann, a young man whose hard-drinking youth has finally caught up with him in his early twenties. Here Toren finally reveals the extent of the problem to his friends and family, tracing the damage it has caused in his personal and academic life and admitting just how serious the problem has become.

In the follow-up essay, Toren's mother, Chris, expresses her reaction to reading Toren's e-mail and learning that he is entering an alcohol treatment program. Here she reacts to the troubling news about her son's condition by questioning her competence as a mother (How did she miss the signs? What could she have done to prevent Toren's problems?) and by examining her own alcohol use, especially in the context of her son's addiction and potential recovery.

Chris and Toren Volkmann are the authors of From Binge to Blackout: A Mother and Son Struggle with Teen Drinking. *Both are frequent speakers on the relationship between alcohol addiction and family dynamics.*

Toren

Paraguay, May 21, 2003. A long night of drinking used to make me tired . . . now it makes me stay up and shake. I'm an alcoholic. I guess drinking like an alcoholic for about eight or nine years was part of the problem. Luckily, it was fun as hell.

Now what? Cocaine? How can I find a new identity when I used to drink mine by the fluid ounce and then turn around and juggle reality?

I thought the problem with being an alcoholic was you just drank a lot. I did that just fine and things were great. No one ever said, "Dude, you're gonna start losing your money, your memory and, above all, your longevity and tolerance . . . ," as if just being shit-faced and happy every night weren't enough, ". . . and when you stop a mean bender you're going to be a fevering, shaky, paranoid halfwit for a day or two who can't think, sleep, relax, or even eat until withdrawals are over. . . ." That page of my D.A.R.E. book must have been ripped out, right after the one part I do remember that said the bad guys always had fun and got all the chicks.

I used to be able to handle the worst of hangovers, wear it like a soldier wore a uniform, or drink it off. I could deal with hellacious sleeplessness from drinking for a day or through the night, maybe ending up in some random bed and still charging through class, ball practice, or family happenings like the dark angel that I was . . . even the torrential blackouts that would be reported or random acts of split personality. My friends and I always gave ourselves alternate drinking names (mine was Poren), as a joke, saying, "So and so did that, not me." It was nothing to be ashamed of in the glory days. Things are changing, and what I once thirsted for and sucked on with the finest appreciation, shared with the warmest of friends in the best and most f---ed-up times, is beginning to scare me.

Defining the Problem

The problem isn't controlling my urge to drink; it's what happens to me now when I drink. (Twenty-four pack, where are you?) What was once all benefit and reward—raging parties, boring conversation turned into passionate arguments, blaring

music and endless cigarettes, slurring exchanges of understanding (or even unfaithful or unwarranted kisses)—now
seems to be packaged with much more unpredictability. I now
have a harder time controlling how much I drink and how
drunk I get.

Even more disturbing are the terrible physical reactions,
depending on the amount of alcohol I consumed and my
eventual detox. This is the big problem. During detox, inside
the unsettled body, a nervous and sometimes nauseous sense
begins . . . an anxiety and almost a fear, like being too alone.
You see yourself and everything differently. Like a sudden col-
lapse of the stock market in your brain and every single nerve
ending throughout your body wants to turn inside out and
puke out some unidentifiable pain or itch. You sweat, and you
sweat increasingly when you let unreasonable thoughts trick
you into feeling like whatever you are thinking must be true,
like for example, "this is normal," "this will never end," "I de-
serve this," or "hhhhmm . . . maybe another drink will solve
the problem."

Living for the Weekend

Each summer, I returned from college in San Diego to my
home in Olympia, to live with my folks and work by day as a
groundskeeper. But really, I lived for the weekends, and everything worked out perfectly that way. I would go up to Seattle
and rock all weekend, hardly eating and just shooting the shit
(loving it always), cracking beers from the early morning and
turning over what was remaining from the previous night.
The weekends were endless parties, fiascos, adventures. And
always intoxicating.

That last summer at home, I grew to dread Monday mornings at work, and sometimes Tuesdays, too. It wasn't due to a
headache or hating the job. I liked being outside and listening
to all the jack-offs on talk radio with their big opinions and
constant advertising. But more and more, I would feel ex-

hausted. Sunday or Monday nights I would find myself in bed at nine or ten P.M., knowing that I may not get to sleep until four, five, or six A.M. My legs would cramp sometimes, or ache, depending on how bad it was, or how much I had drunk. I'd have sweaty, sudden convulsions just as my body began to relax or fall asleep. I would be scared to fall asleep and would lie awake frightened, having no clue what to do, in total dread until it would finally subside enough to let me sleep. *Hell.* I tried to think it was normal, but I knew something was up. Little did I know it was the start of what I would slowly come to realize was part of my reality. It was my penance after coming off another celebratory binge. Starting out subtly as uneasiness, anxiousness, and sleeplessness, these reactions slowly progressed over the last two years of college.

Surviving College

The first time I ever noticed that I had the shakes and didn't attribute it to lack of food was in 2000, my sophomore year of college. . . . I was not even twenty-one years old. I was trying to fix a tangled cassette. Unfortunately, my hand was vibrating, so I gave myself some wine and was able to enjoy the tape along with the rest of the wine, after both problems were fixed. Buzzed and horrified, I called my brother and recounted to him what had happened, as if I'd just had my first wet dream or some other eventual rite of passage to manhood. He was unsurprised, if I remember correctly, and I think he more or less welcomed me to the club or alluded to the idea of "Where have you been?" That made me feel better, as did the rest of the boxed wine.

I made it through college just fine and, from what I remember, it was the time of my life. I have a lot of really screwed-up pictures, a black book, and valuable friendships to prove it. I became very disheartened with my difficult routine by the end, though. My senior year was awfully tough. Getting blitzed every weekend was amazing, and returning to the dorms on campus, backpedaling, was always a challenge . . . to say the least.

"My Ridiculous Schedule"

I used to tell people, the few who understood, how my ridiculous schedule went:

> Schizophrenic Monday: Inferior to myself, self-worth plummeting, no schoolwork, too preoccupied and on edge . . . easily startled by common things, vulnerable, and self-esteem at negative ten.

> Worry Tuesday: Still fevering, blankly staring at TV, wondering how I am gonna magically execute all that reading, classes, papers, exams (brilliantly done in the end, I must add).

> Whatever Wednesday: How much I really drank last weekend = how I function this day.

> Productive Thursday: Back on track and kicking ass, do it all, I *am* school.

> F---ing Friday: Sense of humor fully restored, all energy and in gear . . . just in time to start the cycle all over again . . . pattern here?????????????

This gave me about two or three days of productivity. So on Fridays I would delve into bliss, oblivion, carelessness, and a state of being that defied concern. One that was mostly impossible for the average student or peer. Satisfactorily saturated, self-sufficient, and in need of nothing more than my friends and my cheap booze (211, forties, ice beers, or maybe some other high-class malt liquor), I was set. I would drink the half-empty leftover beers (wounded soldiers) and I'd wonder about the party-goers who had gone home early, "What was their problem?" Well, whatever those people did, they didn't seem to catch *my* disease. It must be something toward the bottom of the drink that did it. Anyway, I had the best of times. Simplicity—lots of rocking music, companionship, and drinking games (Quarters, Keg Stands, Beirut, Kings, and Dr. Kilabrew). Done deal. No bars or girl chasing, just laughs, craziness, and comfort. Where was the problem? (See Schizophrenic Monday.)

At this point in my life, I wasn't sure if this was a disease or not (they say it is). I chose it and loved it. Now if I choose to drink like I did before, the symptoms that ensue are surely my fault. I am simply struggling with the aftermath of the next good time that I want to have. Why does detox have to exist and be sooooo painful, making me struggle to talk, and even lose my sense of humor? These are the functions alcohol usually eases for people, but now the results are the opposite. It has me totally puzzled and unsure how to explain it, mainly to the ones I care about, and also the ones who may be alcoholics, as well.

Post-College

After I graduated college in the summer of 2002, I moved up to Seattle to live with some old friends from high school. To save words, I again put into action what I did best. I drank—almost every day. No more school, a bad job market, and man, it was perfect. Even better, there were World Cup soccer matches on TV every night to keep me wasted until five in the morning. *Gooaaallll!!!!!*

Eventually I started landscaping, and I still went hard every night, partying. It didn't seem to matter. I woke up with vigor and readiness. I packed my lunch, and then would get stuck in traffic with my music and a cigarette, knowing that I could work, get money, and go home to good friends and drinks. And those were my summer week*days*. The weekends were ten times better, with girls and parties, concerts, or occasional visits to Olympia. There wasn't a care in the world, and I never had to come down.

Sometimes I would start to come down—maybe I didn't drink much the night before or had an appointment or family dinner. I snuck by without drinking or even nursing a few down, and I'd start slipping into alcohol withdrawal. In these moments, with a wet and hot/cold forehead, I'd find it difficult to focus on the task at hand, like remembering that I was supposed to bring something to the car or not knowing what I had just talked about with someone for ten minutes. My inability to recall details was very annoying, and the further into withdrawal I would get, the more frustrations turned into fears, anxieties, loss of confidence and purpose, and even worse, a disappearing sense of humor. This is the shit that makes up your personality, and when it suddenly starts to change or disintegrate, it is freaky and no fun. It seems totally beyond control—purely physical.

Killing Time

The summer ended with the whole crew of friends seeming to have graduated, changed locations, or split up to travel or whatever. I had signed myself up to go with the U.S. government for two years, hopefully to South America. It was not to fight in the armed forces but to serve as a volunteer in the Peace Corps. This gave me several months to kill, and I would almost literally do this.

I spent the better part of September and October of 2002 in Las Vegas, and at times on road trips to the coast—mainly to touch base with all my study buddies, right? My biggest plan was to spend time with my two brothers, who worked in Vegas, and visit friends from school in San Diego. I have tried to recount and distinguish the nights and different trips to San Diego, and it is almost impossible. Invariably we had a blast and I was losing great chunks of each night, either corresponding to (1) how much fun we had, or (2) how much of a jackass I (Poren) may have been.

I drank every night in Vegas, too. It was great. We raged through the casinos, walked down the crowded strip with our sleazy malt liquors and cheap half racks, almost rubbing in the fact that we could do such a thing in front of such "classy" gambling folks. On our better nights, we would then find ourselves at the trashy Gold Spike Casino, giggling and doing penny slots super early in the morning. Luckily, we knew gambling was another issue we didn't need. Besides, every time you give the 7-Eleven cashier ninety-nine cents, you know you get a twenty-four-ounce can of Steel Reserve malt liquor that'll get you just that much more wasted. Where's the gamble in that?

Withdrawal

Soon after, I went to Oaxaca, Mexico, to study Spanish in preparation for my upcoming service in South America. En route, on a layover in Houston one morning, I took desperate measures to put off the impending withdrawal that I knew would be coming after five months of continuous drinking. I made a quick stop at the airport bar to down three screwdrivers (orange juice and vodka). It was worth the twenty-dollar bar tab because it bought me some time before the madness of my detox would set in. It helped me get through the air travel to Mexico City, and later a bus trip to Oaxaca without sweats, memory breakdowns, and the general ineptness that occur during withdrawal. Not that I wanted to see this as a problem or anything.

Upon arrival in Mexico, I was met with the harshest of withdrawals, which magnified everything I have previously described. I spent two solid nights in a hotel, clawing at bedsheets, taking cold showers, and only going out to find water and a banana (hoping not to be noticed or to have to talk while aiming to remember where my room was with all my stuff). After those two days I proceeded to "recover," and basically stayed away from alcohol all but two or three times in the following weeks. The clarity was quick in coming, comforting, and surprisingly easy. I knew my reality was scary.

From this point on, I think something hit me and began telling me "I can never, at least physically, go back to the way I was." I knew that, not just financially, but physically, I would pay for every drink or intoxicatingly good time I would have. Meeting my family for Christmas in Mexico after eight weeks of language class (and some travel, with a few slipups, we'll say) was perfect—a chance to say good-bye before leaving for the Peace Corps for two years. I showed up sober and beyond any chance of withdrawal. My bros pulled in from Vegas with carry-on bags under their eyes and the scent of a great night on their breath. I was amazed and jealous at the same time. But they didn't seem in too bad shape. How? I couldn't have done that.

Backpedaling

The first two days or so with the family were great. I remember sitting with one of my brothers at a table at sunset, watching my uncle and cousins surf-fishing in the shallow waves. We were talking, smiling, sharing a beer, and savoring a perfect moment. How things should be.

How could the situation change?

"Paging Dr. Toren Volkmann. Please report to your own personal disaster called alcoholism—the tremors, sweats, and antisocial symptoms will be right with you." All I needed to do was start drinking.

Sure enough, after a few hard drinks (tequila that tasted like it had been made in a bathtub), the process began to start. Eventually, the paranoid, confused, intoxicated *me* showed up, teetering on the edge of withdrawal. This side of detox is the one that turns a regular conversation into a task. Even if it is with the closest of friends, it doesn't matter. Although they might not notice, inside me is another whole world of pain. The anxiety and difficulty that exist depend on the alcohol levels in my body—either previously consumed or in deficit.

After Mexico, I had one last stint in San Diego before my final good-bye with my brothers in Las Vegas. I don't remember shit for the most part, and even skipped out on seeing some of my most important friends because I was too gone to really care or make an effort to contact some of them. As it turned out, thanks to a stolen disposable camera and Satan himself, some pictures revealed that I did actually see a few of them. Silly ol' me.

"This Was Not the Life I'd Ordered"

That last morning in San Diego I found myself driving to Vegas in a borrowed car with a gal I didn't know too well. We stopped once, and talked about the same number of times. Although sleepless, I knew that my good old withdrawals wouldn't let me relax, so I was confident I would not fall asleep at the wheel. I even let the same CD repeat over and over because I felt too sick and stupid to suggest that we put in another.

The more days in a row I would drink, the more easily these symptoms would surface, and the more intensely they hindered my normal relaxed style of thinking and way of interacting with others. It really started to steal my enthusiasm, my aura, and my soul. I probably could have looked into a mirror and seen the back wall at times, things seemed so bad. This was not the life I'd ordered.

During my final Las Vegas days, I kept a steady supply in me and generally had a good time. The previous months studying in Mexico had made me realize that my drinking situation was worse than I thought. Drinking now emerged as both my problem and my solution. In opportune moments I think I tried to hint to both my brothers that I was bothered by some of the shit that it was doing to me. (They knew what "it" was and what I was talking about. They're my f---ing brothers! But maybe they didn't.) What I was trying to tell them surely didn't come out clearly. In fact, nothing came out conclusively because I didn't want to say it. If the first step to beating the problem is admitting it or accepting it, I guess I just didn't want to beat anything quite yet. Why the hell did it have to be so bad all of a sudden?

The Lowest Point

Leaving Las Vegas was maybe the low point to this day, in my new "dialogue" with alcohol [things got much lower after writing this]. On the floor that last morning, I woke up all too early—which often happens when the body starts losing its normal equilibrium of alcohol—lying next to a girl I really cared for. We may have actually had sex the previous night (if I could only piece together a few simple clues with some certainty). The fact is that I totally slept with her. I was leaving for two years and I knew we should talk about it. Experiencing withdrawals, uncomfortable and unable to sleep, I tried to act asleep to avoid the whole situation, which should have been a memorable good-bye. I didn't know what the hell to say and I felt like crap. It only made me feel worse hiding my problem from her and sweating out the hours that should have been shared between friends.

With few hours left in Vegas, my problem was worsening without drinks (I didn't want to reek of alcohol when my mom picked me up at the airport), and I had to tear down whatever I wanted from our tastelessly covered walls and pack for my departure and upcoming disappearance. My brothers did half of the work for me, I was so worthless. Good-byes are always difficult, but what ensued was terrible. I look back on it with sadness and regret. I tried but couldn't even smile or appreciate our final moments, or express the joy, the love I had for my brothers and my friends. I was too lost in fevers, trembles, and general ineptness, and I felt like they all could see right through it. I was out of my mind. I was scared to leave, scared of what was happening inside me. It was killing me and was all wrong for no reason. My life was supposed to be great.

Eventually, I boarded a plane home to Seattle, my body in pain, shaking, and my legs aching. Behind me, all the way, a baby shrieked as if to express my exact state of being while magnifying it at the same time. I could barely tolerate to sit, stand, think—to live. My mom picked me up at the airport and I played it off legit. It was a tough ride home, trying to read letters about my Peace Corps assignment in South America, making normal conversation that made no sense to me, only wanting to disappear.

I had two days to "relax" and a night of nonsleep, like so many previous nights during those wild Seattle summers, before the symptoms slowly subsided. I didn't even try to start packing for South America, knowing any brainless attempt would just provoke sweaty confusion and stress. I was worthless. I could barely explain photos of my language school and travels in Mexico to my parents, because I was still so affected by the recovery from that latest binge I had put myself through. Why was it suddenly so hard?

In my hometown in early January 2003, with a bit more time before leaving, I wiggled my way out of seeing most of my old high school friends and drinking buddies. I wanted to be sane in my final days before departing for the Peace Corps in order to prepare myself. Yes, by then I had learned what happens when I drink, but it wasn't over yet. Being sober, I was able to find myself and deal with fears of leaving the country for two years with logic and confidence in myself. But departing to another continent by no means left my problem behind.

The question is: What do I do now? How can I make this work? What I can't help but wonder is whether all those famous (dead) rock stars, winos on the streets, or some of my best friends have experienced these same types of things or are experiencing them now. Maybe they just never said so or aren't admitting it. Maybe what I experience is much different from others. But I can't imagine anyone bearing the internal hell that I feel as a result of hard drinking and continuing on without letting others know. How did I not ever hear about this side of alcohol and withdrawal? For me, the silence is over and it is time to start looking for answers. I am also looking for the right cliché to end this—bottoms up!!

Chris

September 23, 2003. For the first time I open Toren's "My Drink" e-mail, forewarned about the content. I sit at my computer, staring at tough words describing our son's struggling and alienation. Even greater is my grief at his silent suffering, his grappling with learning how to detox himself on his own. I recall the times he splayed uselessly on our couch, peering through his own sweat at nature videos. Over and over. And I now realize my ignorance. I feel foolish and inept. I undergo such inner remorse that I cannot move away from the tangle of his words. So I read them again.

A sudden visceral reaction causes me to detest alcohol. I wish to remove it all from our house. At the same time, I want to pour myself the largest glass of scotch in the world and gulp it down as fast as I can. I hate what alcohol has done to our family. And I worry about Toren's brothers, if they may be in the same gurgling boat.

The next day, by the time Don [my husband] returns home, Toren calls again from Washington, D.C. He is trying to make a decision about his treatment and wants us to talk to Carl, a counselor assigned to him by the Peace Corps. Carl connects us for a telephone conference with Toren. We're talking together as if we are executives making a touchy policy decision. With our boys' grinning pictures splashed on desktops and shelves, my husband and I speak on separate phones in our home while we decide where our youngest should be sent. Carl tells us the team has been assessing Toren's level of disease and informs us that Toren has been classified as an alcoholic.

Did We Know?

"Of course, you knew he was an alcoholic," Carl states.

Did we? I want to say, no, no, we didn't. We're shocked. But Carl has already moved on. Doesn't Carl know we have hardly lived under the same roof with our son for five years? How could we "know"? Maybe we did. I'm trying to defend myself and be agreeable all at once. There isn't time to decide whether I knew or not. I must have known. He's my son, isn't he?

And then Carl emphasizes, "If ever Toren is to return to the Peace Corps as a recovering alcoholic, he must first stay sober for three years." In a matter of seconds, Toren has evolved from slick college-grad volunteer to a failing alcoholic, and now suddenly Carl is calling Toren a *recovering* alcoholic. It's like a miracle. Toren's *already* recovering before I even perceived he *was* an alcoholic!

Three years. It sounds like an eternity to not drink alcohol. Don and I drink it several times a week. I picture Toren going three years without it and I can't imagine it. This Carl must have high hopes. And before I can catch my breath, he goes on to say that Toren is eligible for inpatient therapy (with a success rate of 80 percent after one year), or he could do outpatient therapy (with a 20 percent success rate after one year). Carl maintains that Toren is ahead of the game because he already acknowledges that he's an alcoholic. He is motivated, he turned himself in. Most of Carl's clients, he says, have to be hauled into rehab kicking and screaming. I don't hear any sounds from Toren. Maybe he's sitting there tied up. It's just Don, me, and Carl talking about Toren as though he were a hunk of concrete. We go on to discuss the rehab facility recommended by Carl, which Carl says is not a lockup facility—it's spiritually based and twelve-step–oriented, and there's a Family Education Program. Such amenities. I'm thinking all this time, *What am I going to tell my mother?* And did Toren have a window or an aisle seat on his plane flight out of South America? For some reason I don't feel like cooperating. If I don't, maybe Carl will go away and I won't have to hear all this wrenching news. Carl won't want to work with me. He and Toren can figure it out without me. It's hard to concentrate on all this information.

No Going Back

Carl tells us that Toren thinks he's at a nine-out-of-ten level of awareness in understanding his alcohol problem, whereas Carl maintains Toren is actually at a level four out of ten. Toren listens to all this as we yak about him, and I wonder if he wants to add anything. Maybe he's still on Valium. I strain to hear his breathing. He must be amazed at how, just two days ago, he was digging roots in South America, and now is in D.C. talking on the phone to his parents and an addiction expert. Carl has been doing this sort of thing for fifteen years, and tells us he "puts away" about twenty-five people a year. He has about one person every three years who turns himself in, like Toren; the rest have to be wrestled in.

Carl is very professional, and I can tell he's trying to let us down easy when he breaks the news that, most likely, Toren will be discharged from the Peace Corps. But here Toren cuts in, "Wait a minute. I'll do the rehab, but let's not close the doors on returning to South America!" He sounds agitated, determined.

But Carl retorts that they've already tried sending people back to the Peace Corps in the past. It has never worked because the job is too isolating and there's not enough support for recovery. "Recovery"—there's that word again—is such an optimistic term. I wonder how Carl can throw it out there so easily, before our son has even started. I'm barely used to the fact that Toren's an alcoholic. How can I even begin thinking of his recovery? But maybe Toren's recovery is already starting, now that he's sought help. I try to be optimistic. I want to co-operate with Carl.

"Liquor in South America's too cheap and too available. Toren would plummet," Carl warns. He says not to count on Toren going back before three years of sobriety.

Toren asserts that he still wants to return to his project. He maintains that just because the Peace Corps has tried re-turning people unsuccessfully in prior years doesn't mean it won't work with him. He's positive that he will succeed. It's quiet a few seconds before Toren says, "Okay, I'll go into inpa-tient therapy. But I want to have a discussion *afterward* about returning to Paraguay."

Carl responds to us and to Toren by saying, "I don't want Toren going into rehab focusing on returning to South America. Instead, Toren needs to focus on alcohol addiction and his disease and learning what to do about it. He needs to meditate, to gain spirituality." Carl won't budge.

From my end of the phone connection I can tell that Toren is fuming about abandoning Paraguay but is resigned for the present. "I don't have a choice at this point," Toren concedes. "I'm going to rehab." He chuckles and I wonder what could possibly be amusing.

Making a Deal

Toren agrees to sign a contract saying that if he decides to quit the program, he will contact Carl first. Carl will make the final recommendation on Toren's status after the twenty-eight-day program, and reminds us again that if Toren can stay so-ber for three years, he could have a chance to reenter the Peace Corps one day. He wants Toren to begin the rehab pro-gram on Thursday, September twenty-fifth. Tomorrow. Carl feels we shouldn't waste any time. Toren will be driven there.

We won't hear from him for over one week. If Toren has problems, he'll call Carl. The first week is very hard, apparently.

What could be hard about one week in comparison to the last nine months of hell that Toren went through?

Don and I hang up and rush to one another. It's worse than we'd thought. We had no idea. Or did we? How could we have missed it?

"I'm not going to drink while Toren's in rehab," I announce to Don. "I want to support him."

"Okay. I'll do it, too," Don says. And suddenly we both recognize that there'll be no wine with dinner this evening. No gin and tonic on the end of the dock at sunset. Even though it's Wednesday and we don't drink during the week, maybe tonight we would have, since it was such a stressful day. But we've made the decision. And that's final. If we can't do this for twenty-eight days, how do we expect our son to do it the next three years?

I have symphony rehearsal anyway. And wouldn't you know, after rehearsal, a friend invites me out for a beer. She and I have performed in the viola section for twenty years. We're string player nerds, but usually we go out once every six weeks. I tell her yes, and when we sit at the bar and I order a soft drink, she asks me, "Chris, are you okay?"

And now I understand how the next twenty-eight days will go. I want to say, "Yes, I'm fine. I'm not drinking because I'm supporting my son in rehab."

But I remember that Toren has asked us to keep this news in the family; he wants only his brothers and us to know about it. "Because," he conjectures, "maybe when I finish rehab, I'll go back to South America and no one will know I left."

I blunder through my fizzy non-mood-altering drink. Yet my fellow musician senses my malaise. She knows me too well. I steer all conversation away from our family, hoping she won't ask how Toren's doing. We talk about her kids, her classroom where she teaches, the music for the upcoming concert. Soon it's time to leave. I wonder how I will ever survive twenty-eight days of deceit with my friends. I will be forced to lie.

Getting to This Point

The next month cannot pass too quickly for me. On Saturday it's eighty degrees, most unusual for late September in the Pacific Northwest. Our bay waters are a sublime blue and Don is out in the early morning setting crab traps for our dinner. We will eat alone on our beach before a fire and talk about Toren, our family, and our life in this intimate universe of missteps and giant leaps.

How can all these footprints, one after another, have led to this? I remember as a child I often played Mother, May I? in the backyard with my sisters and neighbors. There were many kinds of maneuvers we invented to get to the finish line: banana steps, scissor steps, baby steps, giant steps. And sometimes we tried to cheat, to get away with something if we thought we could. If we made it across the line before anyone else, we won. Somehow, we got there. It was a game of chance, of contortion. Of surviving the best way we could.

Don and I call Toren's brothers. Toren has asked us to let them know. Even though he wants to call them himself, his phone calls are limited. "Your brother isn't in South America," we begin. And we spit it out about Toren's alcoholism.

"Are you sure there isn't a mistake?" one brother asks from Alabama, where he's in grad school. Twenty-six years old, he had visited his younger brother in his Paraguayan village just two months prior. Certainly he would have sensed this overwhelming problem. We tell him it was Toren's own idea to confess. He listens to us and doesn't say much, realizing that what's happening will not be changed by a brother's opinion.

After the next call, to the oldest, our twenty-seven-year-old son, who lives in Nevada, we are finished informing . . . for the time being.

Each of us must learn the news and sort through the facts of Toren's disease for ourselves. Toren has decided to go into an inpatient rehab program, and none of us has lived in his skin. We cannot tell him whether it is right or wrong. Both brothers will soon read Toren's "My Drink" composition on an e-mail attachment. I want to ask them what they think about Toren's pleas, the time he said he had hinted to them about his distress. But we're raw now. We can't talk about this yet. All of us are waiting for more information, waiting to examine ourselves more closely. And it looks like what Toren has set in motion will pull us right along with him. We're brewing up our own plans for rehab.

Home Is Where the Booze Is

Natasha Charles

Parents of teenagers struggle with whether, or to what extent, to get involved with their children's social drinking. Some parents believe that it's preferable to host drinking parties, where at least they'll be able to monitor whether drinking and associated behaviors get out of control, instead of turning a blind eye to the activities their children might be involved in elsewhere.

In this essay, Natasha Charles, the mother of a fourteen-year-old son, allows him to drink in moderation at home with his family. Charles's attitude is that parental oversight is the best way to teach responsibility. However, she questions the wisdom of a friend's decision to host a party where alcohol consumption is not only allowed but encouraged—where drinking is the main event. Charles's description of the party indicates that she believes there is a difference between her own attitude toward teens' alcohol consumption and that of her friend.

Natasha Charles is a parenting specialist whose writing has appeared in numerous publications and whose interviews and features have appeared on several British television news shows. She produced a one-hour documentary on teenage drinking titled Teen Binge Britain.

In my 14-year-old's circle of friends, it is often the parents who provide a drinking environment, and even supply the alcohol. To include booze or not at a 14-year-old's party—to my mind something that should not even be discussed—turns out to be quite a difficult decision for a lot of parents, especially those who put being their child's best friend above discipline.

Take what happened a few weekends ago, when I kept a mum company while she hosted a party for 25 14-year-olds.

This mother had no qualms about including alcohol. The invitation read: "Let my mum know if you can drink and if so bring some." I received a phone call from another parent who was not happy. Like most of us, she seemed unconcerned about a small amount of drinking at a special occasion or included with Sunday lunch. But she did not like the idea of a party where alcohol was to play a starring role.

On the way to the party, I asked my son if he wanted to take a bottle of wine. He declined then retracted, saying he supposed he would if others were drinking. Reluctantly, I bought a bottle of white wine. I did not want him to be embarrassed and besides, I was looking forward to a drink at the party myself.

As for my son, he would have been just as happy with a glass of coke. At one point during the party he said he was going to another friend's house, as they were the only two not drunk and he was bored. Later he did drink a couple of glasses of wine.

Consequences

By 10.30 PM the consequences of my friend's drinks policy were all too obvious. Everywhere I looked there was someone vomiting. I wondered what their parents would be thinking if they knew their children were quite so drunk. They had, after all, supplied the booze.

This was not my son's first or last experience of alcohol. He had been asking me if he could get drunk for a few months. I have always allowed a little wine with a meal (which is usually left undrunk). I did not, however, want to condone getting drunk. Nor did I want to encourage secret drinking by forbidding it.

I was aware that, given the opportunity, he would drink himself drunk and eventually the day came at a get-together at home. I noticed his glass was always full. I gave him lots of glasses of water and suggested he take it easy. But I left him to it. Indeed, by the end of the evening he was drunk, and spent the night and the next morning ill. Since then he has mainly declined alcohol, only drinking at that party.

My nephew had a similar experience at 14. Now an extremely cool and popular 16-year-old, he avoids gatherings that he thinks will be simply drinking parties. My son seems to be going the same way.

I should point out that my son is at boarding school. Some of the children who attended that drunken party were full-time boarders who will have got permission from their parents to leave school for the weekend to attend a parentally supervised party. Does the parent whose daughter was lying in the grass, vomiting into her hair, know that it is happening at a supervised teenage party? I suspect not.

Setting a Good Example

Alcohol Concern [an anti-drinking organization in the UK] recently proposed that parents of children under 15 be prosecuted for allowing them to drink. (It would be interesting to know how such a policy could be policed in people's homes.) We all know our teenagers will experiment with alcohol a bit. Does it matter?

Well, with government statistics showing that one adult in 13 is dependent on drink, middle-class parents should perhaps wise up.

It is surely up to us to teach our children to regard alcohol in the same way as the French do. Of course, the French are not exempt from drinking problems, but drinking is something generally done with food, rather than a leisure activity to be pursued in its own right.

But, of course, to do that we need first to control our own habits. A survey revealed the extent of middle-class drinking. Perhaps we should start by disciplining ourselves—and certainly by accepting that it is possible for 14-year-olds to have fun without the addition of alcohol.

Bad Mommy?

Gretchen Roberts

Like many adults, Gretchen Roberts understands the relationship between good food and good wine. As a food and wine writer, Roberts has learned to understand and appreciate great wine, and she hopes her own children grow up to enjoy these pleasures as well. That is why this mother allows, even encourages, her daughters to have a sip or two of wine with dinner; to her, it is the chance not only to teach them the difference between Pinot Grigio and Pinot Noir but also between responsible, adult drinking and the kind of binge drinking that is far more common among young people.

When one Roberts dinner party guest turns up her nose at a proffered glass of wine, however, the guest's apparent horror at allowing children to taste wine causes Roberts to reflect on her whole philosophy of drinking and parenting, as she relates in the following essay.

Gretchen Roberts writes about wine and food for Cooking Light, Better Homes and Gardens, Wine Enthusiast, *and other publications. She also blogs about wine at the www.slashfood .com. She is the mother of two daughters and lives in Tennessee.*

We sit down to dinner with friends. I've tossed a spinach salad with dried cherries, blue cheese and balsamic vinegar, and baked homemade rolls to go with the grilled New York strips and bittersweet chocolate mousse. We've already passed around champagne glasses brimming with a sparkling California rosé while snacking on artichoke appetizers, but I smell trouble when Amy declines hers as if she's been offered a rotting carcass by the dog instead of a 91-point bubbly brimming with strawberries and sunshine.

At the table, my husband opens a Zinfandel I brought back from a trip to Lodi, California. The wine's deep fruitiness will, I'm sure, please even the apparently unrefined palates of our friends.

"No, thank you." Amy turns her head again as if my husband were passing her a *Playboy* opened to the centerfold. He hesitates, then sets the glass down in the middle of the table, thinking she might change her mind. "I just don't like alcohol," she says, wrinkling her nose. "It's just a personal preference."

Just a Taste?

"Mom, can I try it?" One of her middle school–age boys looks hopefully at the wine.

"*No*." She is adamant and horrified.

Is she worried we might think she is a bad mother if she says yes? Or is she against allowing her kids to sample alcohol?

"He's welcome to have a sip as far as we're concerned," I say, playing the good hostess.

The boy brightens. "Please, mom?"

"*No*." She saws at her steak with a vengeance.

I'm embarrassed, because I gave my five-year-old, Kate, a taste of my bubbly in the kitchen as Amy and I stood chatting. I wonder if Amy is thinking of going straight home and calling Social Services. We do live in the Bible Belt, after all, where the joke is that Jews don't recognize the Messiah, Protestants don't recognize the Pope, and Baptists don't recognize each other in the liquor store.

Going to Extremes

Nationwide, Americans succumb to extremes, and to excess. We weigh the spectrum from morbidly obese to morbidly anorexic. We eat fast food every day, or only locally-grown, organic fare. We binge drink, or we abstain altogether.

Our country has a stormy history with alcoholic beverages, from the saloons of the Wild West to the bootlegging of Prohibition. Even now, the tenuous post-Prohibition ceasefire still harbors a deep-seated horror of alcohol in general (witness the absurd blue laws), and a special fear of exposing our children to alcohol.

This self-righteous attitude is a touchy trigger for adolescent binge-drinking. Throughout history, children have been inexplicably drawn to the forbidden. When they hear all their lives (while we're feeding them Oreos, Goldfish, and hot dogs) that alcohol is one of the very worst things you can put into your system, they quite naturally want to try it out for themselves. According to the U.S. Substance Abuse and Mental Health Services Administration, 10.1 million twelve-to-twenty-year-olds use alcohol, and almost half of those binge-drink.

In another recent report on binge drinking, British psychology professor Adrian Furnham suggests that parents play the central and the most powerful role in establishing drinking patterns in their children. Parents usually plant their feet firmly in one camp or another, either forbidding alcohol altogether and preaching its perniciousness, or throwing parties in their own home for teenagers, figuring they're going to drink anyway, so let's not let them drive.

A More Moderate Approach

I have chosen a different path for my kids, one that winds through center camp.

I write about food and wine for a living. Because of my work, I know a glass a day for a woman, and two glasses for a man, is considered a healthy amount that helps ward off heart disease and a host of other health problems. Because of my work, I also regard wine as a food, as generations of Europeans have done. And I see it as best enjoyed at the table as a complement to the meal.

When five o'clock rolls around, I pour a Vouvray to sip while chopping ingredients for supper. Since they were tiny, our children have watched their parents enjoy a mealtime glass, and even taken sips for themselves as we teach them the difference between Prosecco and Champagne, Pinot Grigio and Pinot Noir. (Sophia is partial to reds, I'm proud to note, and both girls love to clink glasses together in a "cheers" and to try to master the swirl of liquid around the glass.)

I may be a renegade in the United States, but many European parents share my philosophy. In France and Italy, most notably, children are brought up in a food-and-wine culture, taught to appreciate the pleasures of the table in many forms. The French writer Colette wrote in *Earthly Paradise*:

> At an age when I could still scarcely read, I was spelling out, drop by drop, old light clarets and dazzling Yquems. Champagne appeared in its turn, a murmur of foam, leaping pearls of air providing an accompaniment to Birthday and First Communion banquets ... Good lessons, from which I graduated to a familiar and discreet use of wine, not gulped down greedily but measured out into narrow glasses, assimilated mouthful by spaced out meditative mouthful.

Colette captures the key to growing up with wine: in moderation. Just as my five-year-old understands that an occasional cookie is fine for a treat but an entire package in one sitting is not, she also understands that a glass of wine (or in her case, a taste) is a present to be unwrapped slowly and with savor, not an excuse to binge.

Walking a Fine Line

In choosing the middle path between teetotalers and heavy drinkers, I walk a fine line. By making the choice to expose my children early on to the pleasures of drinking wine with meals, I'm making the commitment to lead by example, to walk that line of wine-as-a-food and not cross it.

When I was a teenager and a curious cook, I once sampled my mother's sherry, hidden away in the top cupboard above the stove. It was cooking sherry, cheap and salty, and years of absorbing the heat of the stove hadn't improved it one bit. When caught, I was duly punished. Like my friend Amy, my mother didn't believe in children drinking, so I satisfied my curiosity in secret.

It's true that I'm addicted to wine: its culture, science, philosophy. I compulsively seek out the variety, the vintage, the vintner. The nuances of the bottle are endlessly fascinating to me, and I hope to impart some of that pleasure onto my kids, just as I hope to instill other precious values into their characters. So I raise my glass to the pleasure of wine: wine at the table, wine as a food, and wine as a family.

SOCIAL ISSUES
FIRSTHAND

CHAPTER 2

Drinking on Campus

Hazing

Robert McNamara

According to www.stophazing.org, "'hazing' refers to any activity expected of someone joining a group (or to maintain full status in a group) that humiliates, degrades or risks emotional and/or physical harm, regardless of the person's willingness to participate." In decades past, this activity was usually resigned to harmless (if humiliating) pranks and other hijinks expected as part of the rituals of joining a team, a fraternity, or another club. In more recent years, however, hazing, particularly on college campuses, has become increasingly centered on alcohol use, particularly the consumption of excessive amounts of alcohol as part of these initiation rites.

The following essay is a speech that was delivered by Robert McNamara, a father whose son Jonathan was killed when he fell after consuming large quantities of alcohol during a fraternity pledge hazing. McNamara tells his family's story and urges state lawmakers to pass antihazing legislation in the state of Vermont, where his son was a student at the university. McNamara argues that antihazing laws help provide definitions and hold organizations accountable for their actions, with far more serious consequences than the slap on the wrist delivered to the organizers he says are responsible for Jonathan's death.

Vermont did pass antihazing legislation in 2000. To date, forty-four states have adopted similar laws.

Robert McNamara is a former high school science teacher. He now operates a wedding photography business in his home state of Vermont.

The word seems so harmless. We often use the root of the word to describe a scene that is somewhat obscured by mist or fog. It is often used to define an unsure frame of mind; "I am in a haze. I cannot focus." I am not here to discuss the origins of the word; I am here to tell you about the consequences that hazing has had on my life and the lives of my family. Jacquelyn, Jon's mother; Christopher, Jon's beloved half brother; Dylan, his twin brother; myself; Colette, Jon's step mother; all the step brothers and sisters and the grandparents, aunts and uncles, friends and associates, the list could go on.

Jonathan Sneddon McNamara was born on Nov. 23, 1974 in Burlington, Vermont. He was a twin. His brother, Dylan, was born 6 minutes later.

They were outgoing, fun-loving, normal boys growing up in the beauty of the Champlain Valley.

I remember their first day of school. They were up at 4 A.M. They were ready. The bus came, and off they went, full blast. They were young for first grade but they were ready!

They were involved in little league, sports in high school, student council, Boys State, National Honor Society, class officers. They had the world ahead of them.

1989

Chris graduates and in ten months joins the Marines. By Christmas, he is in Saudi Arabia, getting prepared for Operation Desert Storm.

Jacquelyn and I part our ways but keep the love of our sons above our differences.

The boys share their lives with both of us for the next few years.

Starting a Journey

1992

When it came time to choose a college, the twins picked different schools. They loved one another but also wanted to expand their horizons and then share their adventures with one another.

Dylan picked Syracuse, Jon choose UVM [University of Vermont]. Dylan was into psychology, Jon into medicine.

At that time in my life, I had been teaching at Vergennes Union High School for 20 years. I was taking a sabbatical to finish up my Master's degree. I was to begin in January of 1993.

I was to leave on my journey in August with my wife Colette, and circumnavigate the perimeter of the United States. We were going to photograph and visit the National Parks that I so often referred to in my lessons but never visited. The last time I saw Jon was in our driveway, on August 24th, the day we left. He had hidden a little note. I found it two days later. He said that we were both going on a journey and he loved us very much.

I made it a point to call one of the boys each week. I would tell them about the grandeur of the Redwoods; they would relate the excitement and challenges of college life. Chris was somewhere on a mission in the Mediterranean Sea. He would never make it back to see his brother alive. It still bothers him today.

A Life-Changing Phone Call

We were visiting some old acquaintances in San Francisco on Nov. 20, 1992. My father called me from his home in Michigan to tell me that there had been an accident, Jon had fallen, and that he was dead. Our lives were changed forever.

What exactly had happened? He wrote to tell me that he was pledging a fraternity. I wasn't that enthusiastic about the idea. I at one time, belonged to a fraternity. I had been hazed but that was back in 1966. They don't do the same things that they did to us—do they?

How did he fall? Why? These questions burned in my head as I flew back to Vermont to find the reason and face the upcoming scene of the funeral service of [my] son.

Those people who were in charge and the pledges know what happened that cold November evening on Rock Point.

Learning What Happened

I received a letter from Jon after he died. He apparently wrote me on the day he died and never sent it. When they cleaned out his room at UVM, they found it and someone gave it to me during the memorial service on Nov. 24, the day after his 18th birthday. It was haunting and strange. He said that he was excited that he got an A on a big biology exam. School was great and that he was busy between his job, schoolwork and the fraternity. He said that he has to go somewhere tonight with the pledges. He didn't know where but they had said to bring coats because it was going to be cold. He also mentioned that he didn't know when he would see me again. He also didn't know some of the other facts.

A member of the fraternity had purchased a large quantity of distilled spirits to bring to the pledging event. All of the pledges were driven to Rock Point, which was private property. It was cold, dark and icy on that November evening. It was a little crowded up on that ledge over looking Lake Champlain with all of those seventeen pledges and fraternity members milling about and drinking.

As the story goes, they were putting out the bonfire. Jon slipped and fell off the cliff onto the rocks 80 feet below. It took over an hour for medical attention to reach him due to the remoteness of the spot. He was later pronounced dead at the Medical Center; the same hospital that brought him into the world wrote his final epitaph on his death certificate. Death caused by extreme trauma to the head and thorax region.

The next day the *Free Press* reported that the fraternity said that hazing was not a factor in my son's death.

Was This Hazing?

Vermont does not have a hazing law on record. Today, 40 other states have anti-hazing laws in place.

Was this hazing? According to bill #76 before this committee today [regarding proposed anti-hazing legislation for the State of Vermont], it was indeed hazing.

Section B of the bill states ... "any activity that subjects the student of an unreasonable risk or harm ... " (Taking pledges out to Rock Point on a cold dark evening?).

Section C ... "Any activity involving consumption of a food, liquid, alcoholic beverage, liquor, drug, or other substance which subjects the student to an unreasonable risk of harm or which adversely effects the mental or physical health and safety of the student ... "

Jon's blood alcohol content was .125 and according to the autopsy, was rising at the time of death.

A recent editorial in the *Free Press* claims that we have laws to protect us now.

Three of the fraternity members were charged. Providing alcohol to a minor.

They paid a small fine, and had to perform some hours of community service. The fraternity was put on social probation for a few months—no parties for a while.

Why We Need an Anti-Hazing Bill

If the laws protect us, then why do we need this bill? I can assure you that if I, as an adult, took 17 kids on a field trip, provided them with the availability of alcohol that I had purchased and one of the kids fell to their death, I would not be here before you today. I would still be in prison.

We need to pass this bill. It is clear and concise. It forces organizations to have an anti-hazing plan in place. It takes the "Haze" out of hazing. It educates. It lets groups, organizations, clubs and fraternities know that there are certain things that you cannot do to people. It eradicates the notion that hazing is OK and a part of student life.

This bill before us today will save lives. It will make people think twice before they engage in any reckless and demeaning behavior associated with hazing. It will be clearly against the law to engage in any hazing activity as described in this bill.

I often wonder: if Vermont had an anti-hazing bill in 1992, would my son be alive today? Would the fraternity members have thought twice about taking pledges to an unsafe location and then provid[ing] alcohol?

We need to pass this bill.

It may someday save the life of your son or daughter.

Tough Choices

Elizabeth Miller

In the following essay, college student Elizabeth Miller groups the decision about whether to drink in college together with other tough choices that confront college students, choices like whether to have sex or whether to be dishonest on an exam or other assignment. In Miller's case, her decision is made more complicated by her competing desires to fit in at a college party and to remain true to her Christian principles.

Eventually, Miller found a group of like-minded Christian students who were able to create enjoyable social activities without alcohol. She balanced out her participation in Christian organizations, however, with membership in a social sorority, where she met and made friends with all sorts of students who had dealt with those tough choices in different ways.

Elizabeth Miller attended Miami University of Ohio, where she was a member of the Delta Lambda chapter of the Kappa Kappa Gamma sorority.

A thick haze of cigarette smoke hung in the air of the fraternity house and the air reeked of alcohol and strong cologne. As I squinted through the haze, trying to make out a familiar face, I found myself being squeezed through a maze of rowdy college students.

It was my first weekend in college and I'd come to a frat party with a group of other freshman girls. It didn't take long, though, for me to lose them in the crowded living room. Suddenly I felt very lost and alone.

As a new freshman, I wanted to get the full college experience by exploring new situations on campus. I couldn't wait

Elizabeth Miller, "Party Girl?: I Wondered If Drinking at This Frat Party Would Help Me Fit In," *Ignite Your Faith*, vol. 64, March–April 2006, pp. 50–52. Reproduced by permission of the author.

to be free of midnight curfews and the regular check-ins my parents had required. For the first time in my life I had no one to follow up on whether I was doing the "right things." No one, that is, except God. But suddenly God felt like a weight around my neck. And while I didn't want to throw away my Christian values, I also didn't want to feel like an outsider. Most of all, I wanted to be accepted, and I thought going to this party would help me fit in and find new friends.

Without a beer in my hand, I soon realized I looked out of place. Partiers kept asking, "Do you want a beer?" or "Why aren't you drinking?" My response was usually a meek, "I'll get one later" or "I'm OK for now." I couldn't get myself to actually say I didn't drink, afraid I'd be asked why. If I told them the real reason, I'd end up being labeled the antisocial God-girl who didn't want to have fun. So to keep from having to answer any more uncomfortable questions, I grabbed a can of beer, wedged my finger under the tab and nervously pushed upward.

Click.

Second Thoughts

The can cracked open and I suddenly caught a wiff of its bitter odor. I looked quickly around at the oblivious partiers and then slowly brought the can toward my lips. Before I took my first swig, I heard a voice cut through the noisy crowd and loud music.

"I've never seen anyone inspect their drink so much." I turned to see a guy standing behind me.

I gave a nervous laugh, suddenly aware of my noticeable awkwardness. "I guess I'm a beginner."

"So you're a freshman."

"Is it that obvious?"

"Only because you look like you're about to drink poison."

"Have to start sometime," I said fidgeting with my can, and then saw that he wasn't holding one. "Where's yours?"

"Oh, it's not my thing," he said with a casual shrug.

"You don't drink?"

"Nah."

I wondered if he was serious. "But you're at a frat party, you're supposed to."

"Not at all. I live here, actually. And hi, I'm Kevin."

"Nice to meet you, Kevin. I'm Elizabeth. . . . This is your fraternity? And you don't drink?" I saw a cross necklace around his neck.

"Right. I still go out and have a good time, just without the alcohol. Nobody thinks it's a big deal." He smiled and nodded toward my beer. "Are you sure you want that?"

"It's Not Worth It"

I didn't say anything, and simply put down the can. I immediately felt relieved, but something still bothered me.

"Doesn't it get frustrating always being the only sober person at a party like this?" I asked.

"Not anymore," Kevin responded. "But I used to struggle with that frustration. It wasn't always easy for me to turn down a drink."

"Did you used to drink?"

"I drank once at the beginning of my freshman year, just to see what it was like. But now I've seen what the other side is like, and it's not worth it. Just look at all these people." He motioned to the dozens of people surrounding us who were stumbling around and shouting vulgar things. "I didn't want to be that."

"But aren't you still friends with them?"

"Sure, they're my fraternity brothers, and a lot of them actually respect me for not drinking. But I have other friends outside the fraternity who don't drink. I just had to look for them."

I paused and thought about what Kevin had just said. "Well, I've been looking, and I sure haven't seen many around. It seems like everyone is into the party scene."

"Not everyone is into drinking. Have you ever heard of Campus Crusade for Christ?"

"No, what is it?"

"It's a Christian outreach group on campus," he said. "It meets every Thursday night. That's where I met people who shared my faith, but still wanted to have fun on campus."

"I'll have to check it out," I said, spotting my friends who were signaling me at the door. "Well, I think I'm going to call it a night."

"Nice meeting you," he said with a wave. "Maybe I'll see you on Thursday."

Finding a Friend

The next Thursday night I went to the meeting for Campus Crusade for Christ and I saw that I wasn't the only Christian on campus. In fact, there were hundreds of other students there. Soon I had a close group of Christian friends who shared my beliefs and supported me through tough decisions. And as I got more comfortable with my faith on campus, I started leading a Bible study for freshman girls. But I don't only hang out with people who believe just like I do. In fact, I joined a sorority where I've made friends with girls from all kinds of religious and nonreligious backgrounds.

I still face difficult choices. Sometimes it's about drinking alcohol, other times it may be about sex or cheating in class. Each time I have a difficult decision to make, I turn to God for guidance. As for parties, I now know I don't even have to pick up a beer can to fit in with the crowd. I want to be the kind of person that I would seek out at a party. Amidst the haze, I want to shine.

Twenty-One at Last

Cassandra Keyse

For many college students, turning twenty-one is a rite of passage. They have spent, in many cases, their entire high school and college careers drinking illicitly at parties, in dorm rooms, in secret. Then, at the stroke of midnight on their twenty-first birthday, they are legally able to hit the town, and many do, starting their pub crawl at midnight and wrapping up only when the bars close.

Cassandra Keyse was no exception. When she turned twenty-one, she drank six drinks after midnight on her birthday, only to start up drinking again later that same day. After the hangover had worn off, however, Keyse started to reflect on the consequences of this ritualistic binge drinking on her and other students' lives. She offers advice to others approaching their twenty-first birthdays while remaining realistic about this ongoing tradition.

Cassandra Keyse is a journalism student at California Polytechnic State University.

Twenty-one. It's the age that almost everyone looks forward to from high school on. In fact, it is the last age that is looked forward to period (unless you are among the people who can't wait until you turn 25 so you can rent a car). This is a milestone that is celebrated in the United States by parading the birthday person from bar to bar and buying them way too much alcohol to commemorate their right to legally get intoxicated in public as opposed to in a dorm room, fraternity party and the like. It is the age of ultimate freedom, so why are we so harsh with the initiation?

On Wednesday night, I celebrated my 21st birthday. I went out in the rain at midnight to celebrate as soon as the date moved from March 3rd to March 4th. In the hour that I was downtown that night, I had six drinks, an example of binge drinking at its finest. I got enough sleep to rally for class the next day and then went out again Wednesday night.

Celebrating or Just Surviving?

Sadly, I do not know how many drinks I had in the couple of hours I was at the bars that night. Alcohol got the best of me and I was home in bed by midnight. Yes, it was fun, but I found myself contemplating whether or not I needed to down every drink that was put in front of me. The pain of the following day rendered me useless until late afternoon, well after my 9 A.M. class and the beginning of my shift at work. I had survived my 21st birthday and lived to tell about it, but should I really be content with that? After all, birthdays are happy days, not days to simply hope you get through.

As much as I hate to admit it, my birthday celebration became a statistic. According to a 2008 article in the *Journal of Consulting and Clinical Psychology* entitled "21st Birthday Drinking: Extremely Extreme," four out of five students surveyed admitted to drinking large amounts of alcohol to celebrate their 21st birthdays. To further analyze the survey results, researchers calculated that 68 percent of females and 71 percent of males had a blood alcohol content of over .08, the point at which drinking is defined as binge drinking.

A Dangerous Tradition

As college students, we know the negative consequences of binge drinking and yet so many of us participate in it willingly, continuing this detrimental tradition. I wish I hadn't chosen to sign my night over to an unknown quantity of alcohol, but it was what my peers had done and joining their ranks seemed like the only respectable thing to do.

My view of turning 21 has changed in the few days after my birthday. I have learned that while parts of society frown on the practice of over-drinking, other parts have encouraged it as a normal way to end the 20th year of life. I have accepted my right to buy and consume alcohol, but haven't exercised it since that night because simply, the mystique and excitement are gone.

I am an adult in all respects now and as such, I do not intend to pass on the binge-drinking initiation tradition that so many of us went through. My birthday experience was what I thought it would be; it was fun until the final drink that knocked me out. Know your limit. You'll be thankful in the morning.

Alcohol will be there tomorrow and the next day. Pace yourselves, please.

Battling the Alcohol Culture
on Campus

*Charles Schroeder, an Interview with Robert L. Carothers
and David Hardesty*

*Many college students might not realize that their school's fac-
ulty and administrators take students' alcohol use, and campus
policies on alcohol, very seriously. As the following interview illustrates, many factors come into play when colleges and universities consider how to balance student freedoms with safety,
health, and security. In particular, organizational structures,
community relationships, and law enforcement all need to be
taken into account, as does the effect that student drinking has
on the college experience and on the university's enrollment potential.*

*Here Charles C. Schroeder, the editor of a magazine about
campus life, conducts an interview with Robert L. Carothers, the
president of the University of Rhode Island, and David Hardesty,
the president of West Virginia University. Both schools had recently been featured on the list of top party schools nationally,
prompting the schools' administrators to reevaluate institutional
policy on alcohol and consider how to make positive changes.*

*Charles C. Schroeder has served as student affairs officer at
several universities, including the University of Missouri and
Georgia Tech. He now serves as a consultant to institutions of
higher education.*

*C*harles Schroeder: We are very interested in what you as
presidents have done to stimulate cultural change related
to binge drinking. We're interested in insights and lessons
learned that our readers can explore as they try to deal with
this national problem.

Charles Schroeder, an Interview with Robert L. Carothers and David Hardesty, "Battling
the Alcohol Culture on Campus," *About Campus*, July–August 1999, pp. 12–18. This material is used by permission of John Wiley & Sons, Inc.

Could both of you describe the triggering events or the major impetus for really pushing the kind of substantial organizational change that you have under way at Rhode Island and West Virginia? Bob, do you want to start with that?

Robert Carothers: Well, as you know, we [the University of Rhode Island] spent two years at the top of the *Princeton Review*'s list of the top party schools in the country. This began to affect not only the external perception of the university but the internal perception as well. Students were attracted by that banner, and therefore the problem was growing in geometric proportions. We also had a very surprising and large legal judgment against the university for something that had happened to a young woman in a fraternity house. That $750,000 judgment woke everybody up with regard to our responsibility to students. For a period of time the prevailing attitude had been, "Well, . . . *in loco parentis* ["in place of a parent"] is over; . . . what they do is not our business." The court sent us the message that what students do is indeed our business. This case, coupled with the *Princeton Review*'s calling us the top party school, focused us on the problem.

Schroeder: David, as I recall from a National Forum for Senior Administrators presentation you gave on prevention of alcohol and drug abuse, West Virginia also had that wonderful distinction of being named the top party school in the nation by the *Princeton Review*.

David Hardesty: We did. As I was preparing to take office and looking into matters influencing enrollment, I became aware that West Virginia University had a reputation not only as a school where binge drinking occurred but as a school with an attitude toward students that was laissez-faire ["let them do what they wish"] in many respects. Clearly, this was on the minds of the parents and the students looking at the university, and I'm sure it was affecting our ability to attract students. What did we have to offer? We had residence halls where it was difficult to study and where parties were out of control. In fact, at that time there was one annual block party here that would attract ten thousand students on the first night of class and at which genuinely dangerous conduct occurred. This kind of conduct—assaults and fights and such—was directly related to alcohol. So the upshot is that we adopted a series of policies to address alcohol abuse. However, it's important to keep in mind that these were actually part of a larger set of policies to work toward becoming a more student-centered university. We were trying to effect a cultural change throughout the university—one that we felt would ultimately help us improve recruiting in the state of West Virginia and the surrounding states.

Making Changes

Schroeder: Let's talk a little bit about the way both of you approached making this kind of cultural change on your campuses. Bob, you mention in your article "A University in Recovery" that you encountered resistance that was somewhat unexpected. As I recall, part of it was from the Development Office, which was saying this kind of effort could be bad in terms of alumni relations. So could both of you talk a little bit about any resistance you encountered, maybe some that was anticipated—in the case of Rhode Island, certainly fraternities weren't happy about the changes—but maybe some that was unanticipated and how you dealt with that as leaders?

Carothers: We were building a new culture, and we announced it as such. That was the title of the vision statement we put forth, "Building a New Culture for Learning," in which we outlined a move to a more active and collaborative culture, sort of along the lines of the Wingspread principles [a system for assessing student learning]. It became clear that we were not going to be able to achieve that with a student body whose minds were clouded by alcohol. So that had to change. But there was the feeling from many within the community that if we changed and took a hard line on alcohol use we would jeopardize the flow of enrollment into the university—that we would alienate the alumni whose memories of the university were often associated with alcohol and tailgating at events and so forth. I did run into resistance there. I also ran into resistance from some of the deans, who said alcohol was essential to some of their development activities. And I ran into some resistance, surprisingly, from the town; [The locals] felt that if I shut down drinking on campus it would flush it out into their neighborhoods in a way that was not manageable. They used to say, "You're just going to put a lot of drunken kids on the twisty highways of south Rhode Island."

Schroeder: David, did you experience similar types of resistance or concerns from constituents both on and off campus?

Hardesty: The first thing that I tried to do was to educate the campus about the need for the change. There was not widespread understanding of the depth of the problem and how it was hurting recruiting. However, I think the primary resistance was not really internal as much as from a local economy that encouraged drinking, a problem in many college towns. We encountered the whole advertising culture that invites students to try out and indulge in alcohol, and we encountered resistance from persons who make considerable amounts of money catering to underage drinking. The town in general I think was with us, and there was a feeling that our efforts would benefit the community as well. Among our strongest allies were parents. For example, there's our Mountaineer Parents Club, a student-centered initiative we started and my wife, Susan, chairs, which brings together thousands of family members across the state and across the nation. Together, the university administration and our parents clubs worked to raise awareness of the issue. The student newspaper and the local newspaper reported the changes we were making, got views on the pros and cons, and helped keep the discussion going.

Getting Faculty Involved

Schroeder: Henry Wechsler, when he released his first study on student drinking and came out with his twelve interventions, talked about the need to make the academic week a full five-day week, not a three-day week where you wouldn't have exams or assignments on Thursday or Friday [but one] where faculty would expect class attendance [on those days]. Those kinds of things. How did you engage faculty as part of the solution in this overall problem you were attempting to address?

Hardesty: As a result of our strong belief in supporting students in their first year, we created Operation Jump Start. Faculty couples were appointed to residence halls where our freshmen were required to live, and each couple had to live adjacent to the appropriate hall. We built townhouses near all of the residence halls for this purpose. Each has living space for faculty couples, as well as space for student programming, such as computer labs. I believe there has been too much separation of responsibility, with student affairs responsible for life outside the classroom and academic affairs for life inside the classroom. I see the two as intimately related. The resident faculty leaders, whom our students call RFLs (pronounced *riffles*), have drawn other faculty into the programming at the residence halls. Today you'll find some classes in residence hall rotations. The faculty leaders also plan special trips, tutoring, dinners, lectures, discussion groups, and other activities for students in their halls. This effort, along with a host of others, has led to a revitalization of our freshman experience and, indeed, the overall student experience. Having faculty involved with students outside the classroom is critical to giving these young adults the positive support and guidance they need and that we feel is vital to the kind of behavioral and cultural change we are trying to encourage.

Schroeder: Bob, have you created similar kinds of initiatives or other ways of getting faculty connected to the issue?

Carothers: We put in place a freshman seminar, which we call URI 101, that helps with freshman transitions and with transfers. All the freshmen are required to take that course. We have about eighty-five faculty members who teach these seminars. They are relatively small seminars, fifteen to twenty students, ... and a substantial portion of [URI 101] looks at issues of alcohol abuse and other substance abuse, issues of campus violence, date rape, things of that nature. To help faculty members who may have come from a lot of traditional disciplines prepare for teaching this course, we have offered special workshops and seminars.

It's important to note that a significant portion of the battle over the changes we have wanted to make here has involved the fraternities and their behavior. The faculty have been pretty vociferous critics of that culture for a long time, so many of them came forward under that banner, particularly women faculty who say the fraternities and alcohol abuse is a women's issue. So we had a task force that was formed around that issue, and then we had seminars. I went to the faculty senate and I asked the faculty senate to approve a policy change that banned serving alcohol at any social function on campus, which generated a good debate and discussion.

Community Cooperation

Schroeder: One challenge we face in Columbia [where the main campus of the University of Missouri is located] is a local scene where eighteen-to-twenty-year-olds can get into any bar where there are offers of penny pitchers, quarter rounds, or something beyond anything I had ever heard about before, called "free till you pee." My point is, how do you somehow reconcile the wonderful kinds of educational interventions you're implementing on both of your campuses with the rite-of-passage mentality that we find in many late adolescents who are drawn to these local watering holes with the intent of getting drunk, smashed, blind, whatever you call it. Have you attempted to work with bar owners in the communities to get them to be a part of the solution?

Carothers: Well, we've done a great deal of that, but I've frankly found that the most important thing is to work with the police departments and focus on enforcement. I tell those departments that it is my job to enforce the law in my jurisdiction and it is their job to enforce the law in their jurisdiction and I'm going to hold them accountable for doing that. The downside of that is that they'll make it an issue whenever our students have some big neighborhood party. Still, I think that keeping political pressure on law enforcement around this issue is probably more productive than trying to persuade these people who make huge amounts of money by violating the law that they should do differently.

Schroeder: Since you've implemented this change, has the police department responded differently or come up with new sanctions or new approaches to dealing with underage drinking?

Carothers: I think mainly they have simply made their presence more felt with the bar owners. They know that they are going to be held accountable for enforcing the law. I've gotten the governor involved in this, too. He is an alum and was supportive, so I have tried to get him, whenever I can, to talk about the issue of student drinking when he is in town.

Schroeder: So you've dealt with this or are attempting to deal with it at three levels: the campus level, your community (surrounding community), and actual policies at the state level.

Carothers: Right, and I'm just fortunate—it hasn't always been the case—that I've got a governor who is very interested in this issue and in the university, so he has been very helpful. For example, he is pushing a change in the state law to lower the driving-while-intoxicated blood alcohol level to .08.

Schroeder: David, what is the situation at West Virginia in terms of the issue of town-gown relationships around this problem, and what kind of support have you gotten from your local police and maybe restaurant and bar owners?

Hardesty: Well, the support of the mayor, the city council, and the local police has been extraordinarily good, as well as the Alcohol and Beverage Control Commission, which has exclusive jurisdiction for some of the alcohol-related laws. At one point in time in West Virginia, students could drink beer at eighteen and spirits at twenty-one. This led to the creation of bars that catered to students eighteen to twenty-one, and they were on the whole much safer. The law that moved the drinking age for all alcohol to twenty-one has been difficult to enforce across the nation. As a result, bars that formerly specialized in dancing and beer have added drinks, and you see [their] kind of advertising in all major college towns. Our strategy is to intervene by providing safer alternatives for students. For example, on weekends we have created an alternative to the bar scene, called Up All Night. We provide programming and food for students in the hours they like, generally from 9 P.M. until 2 A.M. Students find that an attractive alternative and actually come out of the bars earlier to eat and go to bed, and as a result we've seen vandalism decline and incidents reportable to the police are down. So the police have been very much supportive. Up All Night and other similar alternatives—like the Fall Fest, which was instituted to replace the student-organized block party I referred to earlier—have grown out of a cooperative effort with students. They essentially designed the events. I think it is imperative that students be a part of the process.

This reminds me . . . one sign we have that the culture on campus is changing is that last year [1998–'99] our student body president was elected handily. Notably, he had never been to a block party, because it has been four or five years since we've had one.

Leadership

Schroeder: I take it that both of you were very active and very visible in working for these changes. Is that correct, that you didn't delegate that down to someone . . . that you took a leadership role?

Hardesty: Yes, that's true. I am identified with these programs, as is the vice president for student affairs, who is a nontraditional vice president. He is an assistant adjutant general of the United States military, a two-star general with a lot of experience in dealing with problems associated with young men and women in the service, and he has been an exceptionally fine leader in putting some of these programs together. Still, we did find some resistance in student affairs. Mostly, I think, it was based upon the traditional role and the philosophical underpinnings of the student affairs profession in the United States. But by and large, I think our leadership in student affairs has been very much a part of the change.

Schroeder: Could you speak for a second to some of the resistance you found initially among some student affairs folks?

Hardesty: Well, the launching of the RFL program brought up the issue of who was in charge, student affairs or academic affairs. To this day we are resolving that issue, and it is beginning to work itself out.

Schroeder: Bob, what about your student affairs folks?

Carothers: The vice president for student affairs is very, very aggressive and supportive, but many people, particularly people who have had the responsibility for the fraternity system, are far less supportive. What has happened here is that the fraternities have not made this transition, and in the last three years we have seen seven fraternities close; one more will close this spring. So we started with sixteen fraternity houses, and this spring there will be eight fewer. They have, one by one, gone down, as a result not only of violations of the alcohol policy but also because they couldn't get people to live in the fraternity houses.

Greek Life

Schroeder: That is an interesting phenomenon, because . . . you've [also] got national fraternities saying [to the houses] you're going to have to be substance free by the year 2000 or 2001. Did you find any support among national fraternity officers and leaders?

Carothers: In fact, Sigma Chi came in here and closed their house on their own. I think that's really still getting rolling. I'm going down at the end of March [2000] to meet with a national fraternity council in New Orleans on this subject, but they've given their chapters a couple of years to make this transition. I have real doubts that, at least at URI, the fraternities are going to survive this transition.

Hardesty: I don't know about the future of fraternities; I have doubts on some days, and on other days I'm somewhat hopeful. We have a fraternity system that is not a large portion of the student body, but I think it is important. In a sense the whole thrust of our program, which is based on making the most of the residential living situation to improve learning outside the classroom, would be a comfortable philosophical environment for a fraternity and a sorority if it were done well—if, for example, there were adult mentors and role models living at the house. Some fraternities did close on our campus because of their alcohol-driven cultures. When they have reopened as dry houses, the pledge classes have shot up as a result of parents' directing their children toward those houses. This effect snowballs as they begin to attract different kinds of students.

West Virginia University has joined a national movement of campuses and national fraternity organizations to address problems associated with alcohol. After numerous meetings, we are now implementing a Fraternity Alcohol Policy that is phasing out the previous policy of allowing fraternities to host events where alcohol is served. Fraternity members over twenty-one will still be allowed to consume alcohol in their rooms or designated common areas in the fraternity house. The policy is controversial for some fraternity members and alumni, but it also has support as part of a larger effort known as Parthenon 2000. This effort already has established live-in advisers at eight of the fraternities, and, as another compliance measure, requires security to be hired and to turn in reports for fraternity events. We have an ongoing committee on alcohol and an alumni support group that continues to implement this policy.

Visible Changes

Schroeder: Having heard both of you speak and having read Bob's article, it seems clear to me, and please correct me if I'm wrong, that you feel you have made substantial progress. You've got a long way to go, but in the video *Be Visible, Be Vocal, Be Visionary*, Bob, I believe you mentioned that after four or five years you really have noticed a change in the culture and expectations and the way folks behave. David, are you seeing similar fruits of your labor? That this is starting to pay off?

Hardesty: Yes. Perhaps the most visible sign of a payoff is the improvement in enrollment, which is what we set out to address in the first place. Instead of declining 2 or 3 percent, it has turned around and begun to climb. We also have seen our residence halls go from an occupancy rate of 82 percent to well over 100 percent. Acts of vandalism and incidents reportable to the police on campus are down. Of course we still have issues to address, but I don't think there is any question that I have less reason today to worry about students actually getting hurt than I did before.

Carothers: I think it is better. I think there are so many complex student behavior issues that they all are kind of run together. However, I think that we can show measurable reduction in binge drinking. We can show that alcohol poisoning cases reported and things of that nature have declined, and as David said, we can show improvement in terms of the attractiveness of the institution by the fact that applications are way up. But it is still pretty scary out there.

Hardesty: I would agree that in the end it is the national culture that is going to have to change. After all, in many ways campuses are microcosms of the larger culture.

Carothers: I think the biggest change is that people are now looking at how many of our incoming students have substance abuse problems. I think Wechsler's last study said 37 percent of entering students are self-identifying as binge drinkers. This issue becomes a lot bigger when you have a major portion of your freshman class already in the middle of it.

Lesson Learned

Schroeder: Let me ask you one final question. Are there some lessons learned from the approaches that you've taken, important lessons for other folks who want to create the kind of change that you've created on your campuses?

Carothers: Well, this may run counter to many ideas about modern management, but I think there are some decisions that you can't get consensus on. You just have to make them, and then you just sort of live through the flak that comes with it. We went for four or five years trying to make this decision and couldn't make it, and then, to be honest with you, I just got angry and made the decision. Then people kind of rallied around the decision, and we rode it out.

Schroeder: David, any particular lessons or perspectives you want to conclude with?

Hardesty: I agree completely with Bob's statement . . . but I also believe that it is essential to provide a solid, rational basis for these decisions and communicate it through public statements and other venues. Our university is a very flat organization. There are a lot of people with leadership talent and intellect on campus. I think it is important to get the rationale out there in the public domain for people to consider, and then many of them will act on their own, maybe being far more innovative than a president.

Schroeder: From what I know of your approaches, it looks like each of you has come up with a consistent message, and people internally as well as externally have rallied around [those messages]. This leads me to believe that maybe parents, legislators, and others are waiting for some courageous leadership to step out and take the risk, to push the boundaries, and to say this is the way we are going to move.

Wet or Dry Campus?

Justine Ciboch

One technique often employed by colleges and universities to curb drinking among all students regardless of age is the implementation of a so-called dry campus policy. Under such policies, all students, even those of legal drinking age, can be subject to university sanctions if they are in possession of alcohol on campus. College and university administrators suggest that such policies provide safe havens for students and help ensure consistency in how campus alcohol policy is carried out.

Manchester College in Indiana is one such dry campus. In the following article, Justine Ciboch, a Manchester student at the time of writing, comments on the efficiency (or inefficiency) of her school's policy on alcohol. In her essay, Ciboch suggests that students are unfairly punished for breaking no campus rules other than the consumption or even possession of alcohol. She offers an alternative model based on other Indiana schools such as the University of Notre Dame and Hanover College, where a wet campus policy is in place and of-age students are able to enjoy alcohol in a supervised environment.

Justine Ciboch is a recent graduate of Manchester College in Indiana, with a degree in English.

For MC's [Manchester College] seniors, the majority of its juniors and a few sophomores, the luxury of being twenty-one or older, and legal, is a blessing during our college years. It is a time for making memories, both good and bad, and deciding whether to take that other drink with your friends or to say enough is enough!

However, Manchester College is a dry campus, which means that there is to be absolutely no alcoholic beverages at

Justine Ciboch, "Wet or Dry Campus?" *The Oak Leaves*, no. 13, 2009. Reproduced by permission of the author.

any time on campus, not even for celebratory or tailgating reasons! This then results in students rebelling and sneaking alcohol into their dorms in hopes of not getting caught or written up.

A "Ridiculous Ruling"

Should MC continue to be a dry campus? There have been many students who have complained and tried to campaign against this "ridiculous ruling," as some students have stated, but all their efforts have proved unsuccessful because MC is still a dry campus. Many students, both legal and underage have asked, "What will it take to turn MC from a dry to a wet campus? How many more students need to be written up and reprimanded, only to turn around and continue to still drink on campus?"

A couple of weeks ago, a few of my friends, who live in the dorm, were minding their own business and having a good time on a Friday night, with the help of alcohol. However, their night ended in disaster because someone caught them and called campus security. From talking to my friends, Jason Bendix, a sophomore who is twenty, Justin Wulf, a junior who is twenty-one and Chris Null, a junior who is twenty-three, they said that a few of the campus security men were rude and a bit forceful with them and their other friends who were there at the time. Campus Security even went through Null's room in search of more incriminating evidence and trying to find students who may have been hiding.

Is this the way to treat our students just because they had alcohol? They weren't being loud or ridiculous and the only thing they were guilty of is having alcohol in their possession. "It hardly seems fair for students of legal age to get reprimanded for something that they are legally allowed to do," Null said. "Especially since we weren't bothering anyone or being loud and running around."

Learning Responsibility

Most notable wet campuses are the University of Notre Dame and Hanover College, which has placed a bar inside its student union as a place to gather and meet up with friends for a drink or two. Hanover students can even purchase alcoholic beverages at a small café/convenience store on campus. Also, when tailgating for sporting events, people are allowed to consume alcohol outside of the sporting arena, but students of age or older must wear wristbands to indicate their legal status.

The way I see it is that by making a campus wet and even placing a designated 'watering hole' prevents rebellious behavior and even some accidents from happening that are the result of secretive drinking and wild off-campus parties. College is the time in our lives where we learn and receive a great education, have new experiences and meet all sorts of people from different social networks and step outside of our comfort zones. Students obtain the ultimate educational and social experience that one can only get from going to college. Not having to worry about getting reprimanded for alcoholic beverages would only make the college experience and dorm environment more enjoyable and instill responsibility among students.

CHAPTER 3

Regrets and Resolutions

What I Have Lost

Lisa Wright

Often the victims of accidents caused by underage drunk drivers are other teens. That was the case with Lisa Wright, who, at the age of seventeen, was a passenger in a car driven by her boyfriend. Both the driver and the passengers had been drinking heavily, and when the car hit a telephone pole, Wright was thrown from the car and injured severely. She remains in a wheelchair.

Wright's story graphically illustrates the consequences of drinking and driving at any age. Wright had to struggle not only with recovering from her physical injuries but also with maintaining a positive outlook on life. In particular, Wright's essay conveys her sense of guilt and anger at herself for allowing her boyfriend to drive under the influence.

I wasn't the perfect 17-year-old high school senior, but I was pretty normal. I was a cheerleader and the president of my class in Birch Run, Michigan. I was a good student. I had a lot going for me, and I was really looking forward to college.

I drank, but I wasn't the kind of person who was out drinking all the time or even every weekend. I just liked to party with my friends and have a good time. Sometimes, like a lot of kids, I did get drunk.

Joe was my boyfriend at the time. He was the kind of person who would often drink and drive. Even though I never drove drunk, I rode with him pretty often when he had been drinking, and it always seemed that everything would be OK.

He lived about an hour away, and one weekend he came up with some friends I had never met before. My girlfriend and I went driving with them, and we couldn't figure out what we wanted to do.

The Accident

Joe had a fake ID and bought some vodka and wine coolers. The truth is Joe and his friends had been drinking before they even arrived at my house. I could smell it on Joe's breath, but I wasn't worried. It wasn't the first time. Pretty soon we all were drinking and cruising around. It got later and later, too late to really do anything like go to the movies. So we just kept drinking and cruising. We ended up about an hour and a half from my town. I think we were looking for a place to play pool or something.

Joe gave up the driver's seat to a guy named Jason. I remember sitting in the back seat on Joe's lap while Jason drove, and I recall that nobody was wearing a seat belt.

After that, I don't remember anything. The police report says that Jason took a curve in a 25 mph zone at somewhere between 80 and 90 mph. The car went off the road, hit a telephone pole, and flipped four times before stopping in a driveway.

Amazingly, nobody else was seriously hurt. But I was hurt badly—thrown straight through the back window. I was rushed to the trauma unit, and for several days the doctors didn't know if I was going to live. My lungs were badly damaged; that was the main concern. After five days or so, it was clear that I would live.

"Something Was Terribly Wrong"

But I was in such bad shape. I had broken a bunch of bones: my shoulder blades, my collar bone, my jaw, five of my ribs. I don't remember realizing I couldn't feel my legs. I was on so many drugs that everything seemed like a blur. It took a couple of weeks to get my head straight. Still, I do remember something was terribly wrong. I asked the doctor if I would be able to walk again, and he just looked at me and said no. I remember how cold he was. He didn't try to make it seem better than it was, and I'm glad. He made me open my eyes and face facts.

One day, a few weeks after the accident, I looked in the mirror and thought, "Oh, God, I'm a monster. I look like such a freak." I had scars on my face; my eyes were completely red. You couldn't even see the whites of my eyes. My face was swollen, my teeth had huge braces on them, and I didn't even remember the surgery on my mouth. They put a hole in my throat so I could breathe. I had tubes up my nose. It was pretty gross—and terribly painful.

For a while I thought about killing myself, but I was too sick to do anything about it. I thought my life was completely over. I thought there is no way I'm ever going to make it out of this. No one is ever going to love me. I'll never be able to get married and have kids. I thought this just can't be happening. It's not me. But it was me.

Slow, Painful Healing

Putting things back together took a long, long time. I went to a rehabilitation center in Colorado. It was really hard, and I was in a lot of pain. I had no idea what was in store for me. Learning to do the simplest things like getting dressed or putting on a pair of shoes was exhausting. In fact, I was so weak that just sitting up could make me so dizzy that I'd vomit.

In Colorado, I was miserable. I cried every day. Joe and I broke up, and that was pretty terrible. But I wanted to go home so much that I kept working super hard, lifting weights, stretching, learning to become mobile in my wheelchair. I went home after three months, even though they wanted me to stay for another month. I made it home for graduation and the senior prom.

When the thrill of returning home wore off, I felt like a stranger in my own house—like I was living someone else's life. I couldn't do a lot of things I wanted to, and I realized that three months of rehab was just the beginning.

Slowly things have gotten better. My parents and close friends have always been there for me. It's now a year and a half since the accident. I've just finished my first year of college, and I'm really excited about getting my own specially equipped van so I can drive myself. I'll be able to live on my own and take care of myself completely without having to rely on anyone else. I'm fortunate enough to have the use of my hands. There are a lot of people who can't say that.

But the truth is I'm still working to be independent. I struggle with it every day. For example, I have a boyfriend, and when I'm out somewhere (I'm always in my wheelchair), a lot of times people stare at me. That really gets him mad, but I'm learning to ignore it. In fact, most of the time I don't even realize people are staring.

Appreciating Life

Of course, there's nothing in the world I would want more than to be able to walk again. And yet, a lot of good has come out of all this. Before, I didn't really appreciate what I had. I took a lot of things and people for granted. Now, I've gained a lot of compassion for people. I appreciate life a lot more than I used to. In fact, I can't remember being this happy before.

If I could give advice to anyone about alcohol and driving, I'd say don't drink and drive—and never get in a car with someone who has been drinking. You just can't make exceptions. People think that the possibility of being in an accident is so far away—that tragedy is so distant. But when alcohol is involved, tragedy can be right around the next corner.

Learning Moderation

Sloane Crosley

Sloane Crosley's story about developing an aversion to potato chips is told in a tongue-in-cheek fashion, but anyone who's grown up in a culture where binge drinking is the norm will probably recognize her visceral reaction to anything that reminds her of a particularly bad episode. Crosley's humorous essay pokes fun at American young people's tendency to turn alcohol consumption into a competitive game, and it relates her long journey toward being able to enjoy alcoholic beverages as an adult—within moderation. Crosley's story's serious undertones illustrate the dysfunctional relationship many American youth have with alcohol and relates how this young woman learned to navigate the fine line between drinking for pleasure and drinking to get drunk.

Sloane Crosley is a frequent contributor to several publications, including Playboy, Salon, *and the* New York Times. *She is the author of a collection of essays,* I Was Told There'd Be Cake.

If there's one thing for which I have zero tolerance, it's the smell of Lay's potato chips. You'd have more luck waking me up by wafting the smell of those processed starch discs beneath my nose than you would with smelling salts and 100-year-old ether. Which is too bad for Lay's potato chips, because it's not their fault. It's the tequila's fault.

You see, the first time I ever got drunk enough to throw up was at a party my freshman or sophomore year of high school. I don't remember which. This is because I was drunk. I walked into the kitchen and came upon some of my peers doing tequila shots, competing to see who could do more (a funny phenomenon we take for granted, this teenage idea of alcohol-consumption-as-competition). I sat down across from a guy who was sincerely Mexican and who strongly encouraged me not to do this to myself, but I wouldn't listen. This marked the first and last time I would slap my palm onto a table and say the words "hit me." Six shots and two beer chasers later, I grabbed the nearest receptacle—a half-empty extra-large bag of Lay's potato chips—and released the contents of my stomach into it.

But there is comfort to be found in this story. At least tequila, like rum, is a somewhat expendable booze, shining in the summer and pretty much hibernating for the rest of the year. One's maiden voyage on the overdose train is always scarring (I can't eat gummy bears either, due to a lost game of "truth or dare" as a child). A bad drug or alcohol experience can be a taste-altering thing, like a tattoo if tattoos were assigned at random. Or an afterlife in which you are doomed to wear the outfit in which you expired for all eternity. We become engrained with our first grain. It makes me grateful that I wasn't mainlining vodka that night.

Even so, at the age of 14 (Or 15? It's anyone's guess, really), it seemed more prudent to develop an aversion to potato chips than booze. Deep down in its liver, my body must have known it was going to need to tolerate tequila for social reasons. Whereas Super Bowl parties stocked with chips and dip, I could avoid with relative ease.

And my body was right. Now I drink. I am a drinker. At the age of 30, I have grown to love a myriad of beers. One of my closest friends is such an oenophile that she has worn off on me and I comfortably pretend I know things about white Rioja even when I'm not with her.

Wine and beer aside, I'm a Maker's Mark girl in the winter, a martini girl in the summer and a vodka-soda girl when I walk up to the bar and my mind blanks. I make the best French 75 you'll ever have. The other day, I bought a bottle of elderflower (though, admittedly, it feels like it'll be some time before I open it). But it took me an abnormally long time to get here.

Post-potato-chip-bag, I really had to force myself to drink (clearly, I do not come from an alcoholism-prone family and even if I did, I remember hearing my ardently Democratic parents talking about Kitty Dukakis swigging rubbing alcohol and it really frightened me). Suddenly, I was in college and still couldn't stand drinking. Actually, I could stand it, but I just couldn't understand it.

It wasn't peer pressure that drove me to keep trying so much as it was the variety. There must be something to this drinking business when there are 80 types of cider alone.

But every time friends procured bottles of liquor from beneath their futons, I found myself declining. Perhaps my high school tequila trauma had been so bad, it had spilled over and contaminated other beverages. Why could I not appreciate the subtle fruit notes of Peach Schnapps? Or the simple pleasures of shotgunning a Budweiser can?

I felt the same way about drinking as I did about using public restrooms. That is to say, I felt like I was missing something fundamental to the experience. I will never grasp what other women are doing in there that I am not. Especially if there's no mirror. Men tend to think my restroom speed should be a source of pride. Instead, it just makes me question my own hygiene habits. Similarly, my distaste for liquor did not strike me as morally admirable, but as one more bullet point on the list of things that were freakishly wrong with me. I was not under the illusion that my body was my temple. In fact, all I wanted was to make my body my garbage disposal like the rest of my peers. But I just couldn't.

And that is when I left the country and moved to Scotland. Did the students drink terrible beer? Yes. Were they completely irresponsible with their whiskey consumption? Yes. Did they get black out drunk and pass out in gutters? Yes. But it took them hours instead of minutes to do this, which I somehow found more worthwhile. And they did it while watching football at the pub or eating food, which took the competitive edge off drinking.

Perhaps the act of drinking was simply thrown into an almost innocent relief by Edinburgh's more notorious substance problems. Irvine Welsh's "Trainspotting" had just been turned into a movie, most of which took place in the neighborhoods where we lived and socialized. There's a scene in the film where one of the characters throws a pint glass over a bar balcony and it hits a female patron in the eye. Granted, he does this because he has a violent sociopath streak. And the scene itself was actually filmed in Glasgow, not Edinburgh. But watching that I thought, well—the people I know here aren't so bad as that—and I got up to get another round.

I had learned to love drinking the way you learn to love anything—by letting it go—and by the time I returned to New York, I was legally of age to drink or not drink as I pleased. And the rest is history. History between me and my vital organs.

It's been months since I've been *drunk* drunk. Years since I've been drunk drunk *and* not remembered whole swaths of conversation. But with our holiday calendars expanding and our wallets thinning, you would think now is the time to go out and buy the cheapest booze possible and lots of it. And you'd probably be right.

As for me, I will be standing in the corner, sipping whiskey and ginger ale at my own pace. Because the thing I can't afford is to throw up on candy canes and gingerbread people. I like them too much.

Why I Don't Drink

Meaghan Lane

For high school sophomore Meaghan Lane, the decision not to drink alcohol was a straightforward one. Lane has Type 1 diabetes and a family history of alcoholism, so the consequences of recreational drinking are anything but casual for her. More than anything, however, Lane was convinced not to drink after witnessing the struggles of an adult mentor to overcome addiction to alcohol. Lane saw firsthand the devastation that alcohol abuse can cause in people's personal and family lives. Lane's essay brushes aside common concerns over peer pressure and popularity to focus on health and family concerns.

At the time of writing the following article Meaghan Lane was a student at Westhill High School in Syracuse, New York.

Teens are often viewed as young, naive, and oblivious to the dangers of underage drinking and binge drinking.

In many cases, the stereotype is true, and countless high schoolers' weekends are spent in the company of friends and bottles of alcohol.

In my case, though, it's different. After seeing one of my best friends go through a heartbreakingly painful period of doubt and confusion while her mom dealt with an alcohol problem, I decided I needed to take a stand.

Serious Consequences

Alcoholism is hereditary in my family, so I've spent a fair amount of time thinking over the consequences of getting into what so many of my peers do on a regular basis for

Meaghan Lane, "Westhill Sophomore: Why I Don't Drink Alcohol," *Blog.Syracuse.com/Voices*, March 23, 2009. Copyright © 2009 Syracuse Online LLC. All Rights Reserved. Republished with permission of *Blog.Syracuse.com/Voices*, conveyed through Copyright Clearance Center, Inc.

"fun." In the summer before my freshman year of high school, I cemented a decision in my mind, and have stuck to it ever since.

Having just been diagnosed with Type I diabetes, I would look at the warning labels on my insulin that so plainly stated, "Do not drink alcoholic beverages while taking this medication." I finally realized there was nothing to debate about. Why would I jeopardize my life, one that has really only just begun, in order to have "fun" with people when we wouldn't even remember what it was we did the next day?

The not uncommon possibility of getting drunk, being left to "sleep," yet actually falling into a fatal hypoglycemic coma, is one that scares me to this day. I now know that I don't have to be scared, because I'm comfortable with not being the "cool" one—I'd rather be the healthy and happy one, living the life I want to live.

Role Model

Seeing such amazing people as my friend's mother, who is truly a second mother to me, be changed so much by an addiction she could barely control, was a huge wake-up call for me. She faced her problem with courage and is doing well, but every day is an uphill battle that the entire family must fight.

My best friend and I—unlike so many of our friends and classmates—were lucky enough to see firsthand what the implications of seemingly harmless decisions are before we made those very decisions ourselves with the threat of peer pressure.

As for my friend's mom, she has been such a role model for me throughout the years, and she will continue to do so forever and always. Her struggles have strengthened and shaped her into a woman with more hope and willpower than I could ever imagine. I love her so much, and I thank her for taking charge of the life that has made such a lasting impression on me.

Because of her, I've learned to grow into my own skin as high school has progressed, and I've decided that being part of the "popular" drinking crowd is not at all a priority for me. Instead, I know to put my true friends and loved ones, my wide-open future, and my health, first.

Who cares what the others think? We can only control ourselves, and that's exactly what I plan to do.

Organizations to Contact

The editors have compiled the following list of organizations concerned with the issues debated in this book. The descriptions are derived from materials provided by the organizations. All have publications or information available for interested readers. The list was compiled on the date of publication of the present volume; the information provided here may change. Be aware that many organizations take several weeks or longer to respond to inquiries, so allow as much time as possible.

Alcoholics Anonymous (AA)
PO Box 459, New York, NY   10163
(212) 870-3400
Web site: www.aa.org

Alcoholics Anonymous is a worldwide organization that holds regular meetings in almost every community in the United States. AA's twelve-step program has been the model for other addiction recovery and support programs. The organization's Web site has full-text publications, including AA's basic text and *Twelve Steps, Twelve Traditions*, available to read online.

Al-Anon/Alateen
1600 Corporate Landing Pkwy, Virginia Beach, VA   23454
(757) 563-1600 • fax: (757) 563-1655
e-mail: wso@al-anon.org
Web site: www.al-anon.alateen.org

Al-Anon (which includes Alateen for younger members) has been offering strength and hope for friends and families of problem drinkers for more than half a century. The organization offers support meetings, based on a twelve-step model, around the country. Web site users can find local meetings and order any of the organization's numerous publications, which include daily meditations and more comprehensive print resources for adults and teens coping with a loved one's alcoholism.

Alcohol Policies Project
Center for Science in the Public Interest
Washington, DC   20009-5728
(202) 332-9110 • fax: (202) 265-4954
Web site: www.cspinet.org/booze

The Center for Science in the Public Interest started the Alcohol Policies Project "to help focus public and policy maker attention on high-leverage policy reforms to reduce the devastating health and social consequences of drinking." The project promotes a comprehensive, prevention-oriented policy strategy to change the role of alcohol in society. The project's Web site offers free fact sheets on such topics as binge drinking, youth drinking, drinking age, and alcoholic energy drinks.

B.R.A.D. (Be Responsible About Drinking) 21
PO Box 1021, Clarkston, MI   48347-1021
(248) 842-4021
e-mail: contact@brad21.org
Web site: www.brad21.org

Bradley McCue was a Michigan State University student who died of alcohol poisoning on his twenty-first birthday in November 1998. In Brad's memory, his family and friends started B.R.A.D. 21, with the goal of educating young people and their families about the responsible use of alcohol. B.R.A.D. 21 works with high schools, colleges, and families, encouraging abstinence from alcohol for those under twenty-one and responsible, controlled drinking habits for those of legal drinking age. Archives of the nonprofit's newsletter, including articles on such topics as alcohol use and youth brain development, are available on the Web site, as are wallet cards, magnets, and posters outlining the warning signs of alcohol poisoning. The organization also publishes birthday greeting cards encouraging those turning twenty-one to celebrate responsibly.

The Gordie Foundation

2715 Swiss Ave, Dallas, TX   75204
(214) 823-0235 • fax: (214) 823-0236
e-mail: contactus@gordie.org
Web site: www.thegordiefoundation.org

The Gordie Foundation was created in memory of Gordon Bailey, an eighteen-year-old freshman at the University of Colorado who died in 2004 of alcohol poisoning following a fraternity hazing ritual. The foundation's mission is "to provide today's young people with the skills to navigate the dangers of alcohol, binge drinking, peer pressure and hazing." The Gordie Foundation offers several programs, which include public awareness campaigns, student education programs, and a movie highlighting the dangers of hazing. The Web site offers "Gordie Gear," which include branded items such as backpacks and t-shirts, as well as awareness posters, keychains, and wallet cards outlining the dangers of hazing and the warning signs of alcohol poisoning.

Marin Institute

24 Belvedere St, San Rafael, CA   94901
(415) 456-5692 • fax: (415) 456-0491
Web site: www.marininstitute.org

The Marin Institute is a watchdog group that monitors the alcohol industry's products and promotions and educates families and communities on ways to combat the industry's harmful influences. Current campaigns include banning so-called alcopops (sugary alcoholic beverages) and alcoholic energy drinks, increasing alcohol taxes, and regulating alcohol advertising billboards. The institute's Web site outlines the alcohol industry's marketing tactics and offers numerous fact sheets on such topics as "Youth and Alcohol." It also provides youth leaders and community organizers with resources to aid them in their work.

A Matter of Degree
401 Park Dr, Boston, MA   02215
e-mail: amod@hsph.harvard.edu
Web site: www.hsph.harvard.edu/amod

A Matter of Degree (AMOD) was developed by the Robert Wood Johnson Foundation to "bring campuses and communities together to change the conditions that promote heavy alcohol consumption prevalent in many campus-community environments." Ten campuses, ranging from the University of Delaware to the University of Wisconsin, have developed their own coalitions and programs using the task force's resources. The participating universities must demonstrate a coordinated effort with both the college campus and the surrounding community to discourage heavy alcohol consumption among college students.

Mothers Against Drunk Driving (MADD)
511 E. John Carpenter Fwy., Suite 700, Irving, TX   75062
(800) 438-6233 • fax: (972) 869-2206
Web site: www.madd.org

MADD was founded in 1980 by a mother whose young daughter was killed by a drunk-driving repeat offender. In addition to stopping drunk driving and supporting families affected by drunk driving, the organization also actively works to discourage underage drinking. MADD works with lawmakers, advocating to keep the legal drinking age at twenty-one. Archived issues of the organization's newsletter, the *MADDVOCATE*, are available online, as are fact sheets on grieving, injuries, legal and financial advice, and interventions.

Phoenix House
50 Jay St, Brooklyn, NY   11201
(718) 222-6641
e-mail: Coaf@phoenixhouse.org
Web site: www.factsontap.org

Phoenix House provides substance abuse treatment and prevention services at over one hundred sites in nine states. The organization's Center on Addiction and the Family offers two programs: Facts on Tap, aimed at current college students, and Transitions, aimed at high school students preparing to attend college. Both programs offer prevention and intervention resources for students, parents, and health professionals. For students, the Web site offers fact sheets on topics related to drinking and drug use, a self-assessment tool, and links to find help and support. The organization also offers materials and resources for campus health professionals.

SAM Spady Foundation
PO Box 701, Beatrice, NE   68310-0701
Web site: www.samspadyfoundation.org

The SAM (Student Alcohol Management) Spady Foundation was founded to honor the memory of Samantha Spady, who died of alcohol poisoning in 2004 at the age of nineteen. The foundation's mission is to "educate all parents and students on the dangers of alcohol, specifically high-risk consumption, and the signs and symptoms of alcohol poisoning." To that end, the foundation sponsors the formation of alcohol awareness and education programs on college and university campuses. The foundation has produced a DVD, "Death by Alcohol: The SAM Spady Foundation," available for purchase on the Web site. Archived newsletter issues are also available for download.

Students Against Destructive Decisions (SADD)
255 Main St, Marlborough, MA   01752
(877) SADD-INC • fax: (508) 481-5759
e-mail: info@sadd.org
Web site: www.saddonline.org

Originally founded in 1981 as Students Against Drunk Driving to discourage youth drinking and driving, SADD has since expanded its mission to provide positive alternatives to destructive decisions and to encourage healthy, safe lifestyles. SADD encourages young people to start chapters at their own middle schools, high schools, and colleges. The organization's Web site offers ideas for chapter activities, programs, and other resources for chapter organizers and members. Archived newsletters are available online.

For Further Research

Books

Henry Abraham, *What's a Parent to Do? Straight Talk on Drugs and Alcohol.* Liberty Corner, NJ: New Horizon, 2004.

David Aretha, *On the Rocks: Teens and Alcohol.* Danbury, CT: Children's Press, 2007.

Richard J. Bonnie and Mary Ellen O'Connell, eds., *Reducing Underage Drinking: A Collective Responsibility.* Washington, DC: National Academies Press, 2004.

George W. Dowdall, *College Drinking: Reframing a Social Problem.* Westport, CT: Praeger, 2009.

Karen Goodman, *Safe Road Home: Stop Your Teen from Drinking and Driving.* New York: Sterling, 2005.

Linda C. Lederman, *Changing the Culture of College Drinking.* Cresskill, NJ: Hampton, 2005.

Edward A. Malloy and Mark Goldman, eds., *Call to Action: Changing the Culture of Drinking at U.S. Colleges.* Darby, PA: Diane, 2004.

Hank Nuwer, *Wrongs of Passage: Fraternities, Sororities, Hazing, and Binge Drinking.* Bloomington: Indiana University Press, 2002.

Stanton Peele, *Addiction-Proof Your Child.* New York: Three Rivers Press, 2007.

Barrett Seaman, *Binge: What Your College Student Won't Tell You.* Hoboken, NJ: Wiley, 2005.

Stephen Wallace, *Reality Gap. Alcohol, Drugs, and Sex: What Parents Don't Know and Teens Aren't Telling.* New York: Union Square, 2008.

Scott T. Walters and John S. Baer, *Talking with College Students About Alcohol: Motivational Strategies for Reducing Abuse.* New York: Guilford, 2005.

Henry Wechsler, *Dying to Drink: Confronting Binge Drinking on College Campuses.* Emmaus, PA: Rodale, 2002.

Periodicals

Eva Chen, "Drinking Diaries," *Teen Vogue*, December 2007.

John Dart, "College Presidents Ask Public to Rethink Drinking Age," *Christian Century*, September 23, 2008.

Laura Dean-Mooney, "A Lower Age Would Be Unsafe," *U.S. News & World Report*, September 15, 2008.

Karen Fanning, "An Addict's Life," *Scholastic Choices*, September 2008.

Stephen K. Galson, "Preventing and Reducing Underage Drinking," *Public Health Reports*, January/February 2009.

Charlie Gillis, "Generation Tame: For the First Time in Ages, Fewer Teens Are Drinking, Using Drugs, and Having Sex. What's Going On?" *Maclean's*, April 13, 2009.

Meryl Herran and Christy Heitger-Casbon, "Why Was I at This Party?" *Campus Life*, September/October 2004.

John McCardell, "The Status Quo Has Bombed," *U.S. News & World Report*, September 15, 2008.

Sharon McLaughlin, "Troubling Trends: Teens and Addiction," *Advocate*, November 2007.

Michele Oreckin, "You Must Be Over 21 to Drink in This Living Room," *Time*, April 18, 2005.

Denise Rinaldo, "Young, Gifted, and Drunk," *Scholastic Choices*, September 2004.

Susan Schindehette, "Dying for a Drink," *People*, September 4, 2006.

Emma Schwartz, "A Host of Trouble: More Parents Are Being Held Criminally Liable for their Teens' Drinking Parties," *U.S. News & World Report*, October 8, 2007.

Dan J. Segrist and Jonathan C. Pettibone, "Where's the Bar? Perceptions of Heavy and Problem Drinking Among College Students," *Journal of Alcohol & Drug Education*, April 2009.

Michele Serros, "The First Time I Confronted a Friend About Her Drinking," *CosmoGIRL*, April 2008.

"When Parties End in Tragedy," *Boston Globe*, February 25, 2009.

Index

Binge drinking
  birthday tradition (21st),
    74–76
  experimentation with, 98–101
  good memories of, 37, 38–39,
    41
  parentally supervised, 55–57
  as rite of passage, 82–83
  statistics on, 60, 75, 88
  See also Adolescent drinking
Birthday bingeing, 74–76
Blackouts, 30–31, 42, 43, 46
Blame, 48
Bodily aches and injuries, 39,
  95–97
Boundary breaking, 21–23

C

Campus Crusade for Christ, 73
Campus drinking bans, 82, 90–92
Caretaking, female, 33–34
Carothers, Robert L., 77–89
Charles, Natasha, 55–57
Choices, making, 70–73, 88, 102–
  104
Christianity, 70–73
Ciboch, Justine, 90–92
Colette, Sidonie-Gabrielle, 61
College administration
  community involvement with,
    79–80, 82–84, 89
  faculty involvement with,
    81–82
  law enforcement and, 83–84
  leadership of, 85, 88–89
  perspectives of, 78–79
  student supervision, 78, 81
College-age drinking
  alternatives to, 73, 84
  dry campus policies, 90–92

education about, 82
freshmen and, 70–73, 81–82,
  88
legal age and, 74–76, 84, 90
peer pressure and, 70–73
reduction of, 78–70, 87–88
See also Fraternities
Coma, hypoglycemic, 103
Community involvement, 79–80,
  82–84, 89
Competitiveness, 98–99
Confidence, loss of, 38, 42
Conformity, 70–73, 103–104
Confusion, 44
Consciousness, loss of, 26–27
Consent, parental, 34, 55–57
Consequences of drinking
  bodily aches and injuries, 39,
    95–97
  death, 64–68
  punishment, 34–35
  See also Mental effects; Physi-
    cal effects
Control, loss of, 38, 42
Convulsions, 39
Counseling, 48–50
Cramps, 39
Crosley, Sloane, 98–101
Cultural drinking patterns. *See*
  Drinking habits
Curiosity, 60, 62
Cycle of drinking, 40–41, 44–45

D

Date rape, 30–31, 82
Death during hazing, 65–69
Decision-making, 70–73, 88, 102–
  104
Denial
  parental, 34–35, 48–50